*Putting the
Jewish Rabbi
Back at the
Center of
Christianity*

Yeshua
Matters

JACOB FRONCZAK

Yeshua Matters

*Putting the Jewish Rabbi
Back at the Center of Christianity*

JACOB FRONCZAK

FIRST FRUITS OF
ZION

Printed in the United States of America

ISBN: 978-1-892124-74-6

Quantity discounts are available on bulk purchases of this book for educational, fundraising, or event purposes. Special versions or book excerpts to fit specific needs are available from First Fruits of Zion. For more information, contact www.ffoz.org/contact.

First Fruits of Zion

PO Box 649, Marshfield, Missouri 65706–0649 USA
Phone (417) 468–2741, www.ffoz.org

Comments and questions: www.ffoz.org/contact

For All My Bears

Contents

Introduction

This is a book about what matters. Our time is valuable, so let's get right to the point: What matters?

I mean what matters, *really?*—in your Christian walk, in your life of faith? What gives it substance? What gives it direction? When you dig down all the way to the bottom, what do you find supporting everything else?

Different people might have different answers. The Bible. Church tradition. Christian doctrine. Good theology. *God.*

The list could go on. There are lots of options, lots of things that matter. But is there something that *really* matters? Something, *one* thing, that matters most?

I think there is. And I think that even if we didn't have our Scriptures and our doctrines and our traditions, we would still have it—we would still have the one thing that matters most.

Jesus.

If we didn't have anything else but Jesus, we'd still have a firm, unshakable foundation. Even if we had lost the Bible, the story of Jesus would have lived on. Even if we had no traditions, the teachings of Jesus would still inspire us and shape our spiritual lives in beautiful ways. Even without our creeds and doctrines and statements of faith, Jesus would still be everything he claimed to be.

Everything else—*everything* about our faith—depends on Jesus. So if we get one thing right, it had better be Jesus.

And I don't think we've got him quite right.

By that I mean that most Christians don't seem to know Jesus very well.

I know that sounds incongruous, like a complete contradiction in terms. And maybe I've offended you. But hear me out.

I've been in one kind of ministry or another for over a decade—not a long time, but long enough to see a few things. And as I look at my church, as I watch entire denominations struggle to stay afloat, as I talk with other pastors, and as I survey the broad landscape of Christianity (especially Christianity in America, where I live), I become more and more convinced that our lack of knowledge of Jesus—who he is and what he's like on a ground level, on a real blood, sweat, and bone level—is causing problems that are bigger than we can imagine.

It seems to me that we have built a whole lot of structure, religion, belief, doctrine, and practice around a person we wouldn't recognize if we saw him walking down the street.

I don't exempt myself from this problem, by the way. I don't claim to have complete or perfect knowledge of Jesus. But somewhere along the way, as I tried to sort through all of my beliefs and figure out what God wanted my life to become, Jesus broke onto the scene in a powerful way. He started me on a journey toward knowing him better, toward knowing Jesus as a person and not just as a theological puzzle piece or a set of doctrines to be believed.

Don't get me wrong; I haven't abandoned theology. But in searching for and finding Jesus as a real, flesh-and-blood person, I have found that my faith has become something more than just a system of belief. It's become something more like an adventure.

Or if it was already an adventure, now it's an adventure with a map and a compass.

Or if I already had a map and compass, now I have a destination.

This renewed walk of faith isn't perfect, not by any means. But it's more vibrant and more real and more grounded than it was before.

Why?

Because now the keystone of my faith, the foundation on which everything else stands, the *center*, is not a creed, a doctrine, a church affiliation, a theological system, or even the Bible. It's a Jewish rabbi, a carpenter's son named Jesus, and at the center of our faith is where he belongs. It's the only place he fits.

In fact, I hope to show in this book that if we put Jesus anywhere else besides the center of our faith, or if we put anything else in the center with Jesus or instead of Jesus, we set ourselves up for total failure. We risk absolute spiritual meltdown. We buy ourselves a broken and empty theology for a broken and empty church.

That idea is the backbone of this book; it's the reason I'm writing it—because I believe with everything I am that we need to get Jesus right, and that we will never be doing this church thing the way God wants us to unless and until we put Jesus at the center of our faith where he belongs.

The catch is, in order to put Jesus at the center of our faith, we have to get to know him a little better.

Part 1 of this book chronicles the beginning of my journey toward a fuller realization of who Jesus was and is. Part 2 is a portrait of Jesus' life and ministry, a collage constructed of brief snapshots from the Gospels—a picture that is not comprehensive, but that reflects some of the things I have learned so far on my journey. Part 3 tells where I am headed now and what my journey has taught me about life, faith, and how to follow and know Jesus better—and how these lessons have the potential to broadly strengthen the Christian faith.

And that's it. It's pretty short.

I wrote this book for anyone who wants to know Jesus better, so I've tried to keep it simple. The ideas introduced here are really just *introduced*—they aren't developed fully. To get the whole story, you'll have to read much bigger books written by people who are much smarter than I am.

But in case you want to dig a little deeper and see where these ideas came from and what kind of research is out there to back them up, I have included a few endnotes. I haven't sourced every single idea in this book, but there are enough references to give you a pretty good idea of where I stand in relation to other people who have written on the same subject. The endnotes also provide some places for you to look for more information if you find something particularly strange or new to you. Please keep in mind that even though these sources often disagree with each other, and I with them, they are still great starting points for further study.

Finally, this book could not have been written without the love and support of my wife Sarah, the support and patience of my church, and the guidance and direction of Boaz Michael and the rest of the First Fruits of Zion team. In addition, to all those who gave their valuable time to read early versions of this book—thank you for your feedback. May all of you have an eternal share in whatever good this book might accomplish in the lives of others.

Part 1

The Journey Begins

Crisis

It is not as a child that I believe and confess Jesus Christ. My hosanna is born of a furnace of doubt.

— Fyodor Dostoevsky

It's a good thing to have all the props pulled out from under us occasionally. It gives us some sense of what is rock under our feet, and what is sand.

— Madeleine L'Engle

I was sixteen years old, a freshman in college, lying on my bed in the basement and staring up at the ceiling. The same ceiling that my prayers had been bouncing off for as long as I could remember.

I had asked Jesus into my heart as my personal Savior when I was four years old. I had been raised in a Christian home and been blessed with a Christian education. I had been a leader in my high-school youth group, and every week I played guitar for the church band.

If you had asked me if I was saved, I would have said "yes" without hesitation.

And not without reason. I had sincerely said the sinner's prayer, and I believed in the doctrines of the church with all my heart. I could describe in detail each of the major disciplines of systematic theology; I was "orthodox" and proud of it. I was connected in the church, serving faithfully. I wasn't a great evangelist, but I had tried to get my friends saved.

But when I sought for a word to describe my own spiritual journey, a different word came to mind.

Not saved. Not found.

Lost.

I didn't know what I was doing or where I was going. I didn't know what my purpose in life was.

And the problem, the stumbling stone, was Jesus.

I *believed* in Jesus. Son of God, Savior, Second Person of the Trinity. There was absolutely no doubt in my mind that Jesus had come back from the dead, that the Gospels were true and reliable, that the Scriptures were inspired. I read my Bible. I had most of the best parts memorized. I expected Jesus to come back at any moment.

But I didn't *understand* Jesus.

As an evangelical Christian, I had always believed, theologically speaking, that my faith in Jesus had led to a living and vibrant relationship with him. Perhaps because my dad had an Assemblies of God background—Pentecostal—I even came to believe that I felt that connection personally. I mean a real, tangible feeling. And I think I was right—my relationship with Jesus was authentic, and there was real spiritual vitality there.

But *I didn't understand Jesus.*

So I prayed and prayed and prayed for this door to be opened. I prayed for fresh understanding. I even fasted. But nothing happened.

I pored over the Gospels, word by word. But instead of a living Word, instead of a powerful double-edged sword, I experienced the frustration of running up against a brick wall over and over again.

Jesus just didn't make sense. And for me, without Jesus, nothing else made sense either.

Discipleship

Now, looking back, it's easier for me to understand what I was going through. I knew that I was supposed to be a disciple of Jesus, but I didn't know what that was supposed to look like. I wanted to be a follower of Jesus, but I didn't know Jesus well enough to follow him. I believed that my eternal destiny hinged on whether or not I connected with this ancient person, Jesus, but I didn't know how to do that.

How could I be like someone I didn't understand? The answer was simple—I couldn't.

But how could I be a disciple of Jesus without becoming like Jesus?

I had read the book *What Would Jesus Do?* I lived every day asking that question, but no matter how hard I tried, I couldn't find the answer.

I tried to picture Jesus in my mind, tried to figure out how he would act if he were living my life instead of me. It didn't work. I didn't have enough information to fill in the picture.

I wished I could have been one of the twelve disciples Jesus called during his earthly ministry. I tried to imagine what it would have been like to follow Jesus across the rolling hills of the Galilee, enraptured by his spiritual insight, studying and practicing his teachings. But the picture was fuzzy and faded away.

I tried again and again to recreate that picture by reading the Gospels, but it didn't work. I would open Matthew or John and find that a few minutes later my eyes were just rolling over the words, not understanding, not comprehending. Jesus just didn't register; he didn't compute; he didn't make sense. Maybe I knew the gospel stories so well that I had a hard time reading them with fresh eyes. But I think the problem was bigger than that.

Something was missing.

Somehow, as impossible as it sounds, Jesus was missing.

I didn't have a concrete idea of what Jesus was like, but I needed something—I couldn't keep moving forward with a Jesus-shaped hole in my life. So I began to fill that hole with my own ideas. I called it discovery, learning, and growth, but in hindsight, it's obvious now that I was slowly creating my own personal Jesus.

My Jesus wasn't totally fictional; he was based on things I knew to be true about Jesus. For example, I knew that Jesus had changed the world. I knew that Jesus was a holy man. And I knew that he was hard to understand. So I created a mental picture of Jesus based on these traits: an unpredictable, mystical, seemingly random agent of change; an intensely holy man who couldn't be touched by anything impure or secular.

As time went by, I began to work toward that picture—I tried to become what I thought Jesus was like. And while this filled that Jesus-shaped hole for a while, I was left wanting more.

I knew I was still missing something. I wanted to find my way. So I dropped out of music school and enrolled in Bible college. I was sure that I would find answers there.

College

If anything, Bible college was worse than the state university I had been attending. I met a lot of other believers at Bible college, but none of them seemed to be on a better path than the one I had been traveling. The dedicated, on-fire, super-spiritual believers; the ultra-sanctified holy environment; the place in which I had thought I would find Jesus—Bible college didn't provide any of those things. Maybe my expectations were too high, but I had no way of knowing that at the time.

I was searching for something. Most of the other kids there seemed to think that they had found it. But what they had found wasn't Jesus—at least not in the way that I wanted to find Jesus. I may not have known quite what I was looking for yet, but I knew enough to know that none of my classmates had found it either.

These kids knew theology as well as I did. They could answer any kind of question about the Bible. But they weren't the kind of disciples I had hoped to meet. It seemed to me that Jesus was as far away from my classmates as he was from me. We were all full of knowledge, but knowledge wasn't enough. I wanted more.

I thought an encounter with the real, living Jesus was supposed to change a person. It was supposed to turn a regular human being into something else. But I had yet to meet someone who appeared to have crossed over into that kind of life. I had yet to meet a "little Christ." The other students were just regular people like me. The student leaders seemed to be completely absorbed in school discipline; they were always giving the rest of us pink slips for various infractions of the school's code of conduct. The staff and administration were mostly inaccessible.

We had mandatory prayer meetings every night. Only a few students seemed to take them seriously. They were good people.

They're still good people. And good disciples. We keep in touch. But if they had come to Bible college to find Jesus, I was sure that they were just as disappointed as I was.

The beginning of each semester featured mandatory revival meetings, but there was never any revival. It seemed ridiculous to think that making kids attend more church would create some kind of spontaneous spiritual awakening.

I spent two semesters at Bible college, and the entire year felt empty and fake. I was left wondering—Is this it? Is this the Christian experience? Is this what it means to have a relationship with Jesus?

Russell

I left Bible college behind at the end of my sophomore year and transferred to an online program somewhere else. I wasn't quite ready to give up, but I felt like I was running out of options. After all, if I couldn't find Jesus at Bible college, then what hope did I have?

I was still young enough that it didn't feel weird to move back in with my parents. My mom, an Air Force colonel, had just been stationed at Langley, right on the Chesapeake. We could see the water from our house. It was nice.

I connected with a few small churches there, one of which offered a Saturday night service that catered to young airmen—eighteen-to-twenty-somethings who had entered the service right out of high school. Kids my age, most of them. One airman introduced me to a friend of his, a media consultant named Russell. Russell was knowledgeable, jovial, and most of all, kind.

Russell wasn't Jewish, but he wore a Star of David necklace.

I had been raised as a dispensationalist. Dispensationalists brought a love of Israel and the Jewish people into the mainstream of American Christianity. If you've ever seen an Israeli flag or a shofar (a sort of trumpet made from an animal horn) or a Passover Seder plate at a church or in a Christian home, you've seen the influence of dispensationalism.

Dispensationalists predicted the establishment of the modern State of Israel half a century before it happened. They have always believed that the Jewish people still have some part to play in God's program. So as a dispensationalist, I was excited to meet another believer who loved Israel and the Jewish people.

In the course of conversation, it came out that Russell kept kosher. I don't know how he did it on an Air Force base, eating cafeteria food. But as far as I could tell, he followed the dietary laws of Leviticus 11.

I had been taught my whole life that following these laws was unnecessary. I had proof texts and Bible verses memorized from years of attending Bible classes. So I told Russell that he didn't have to restrict his diet. "Jesus fulfilled the Law," I told him. "So you don't have to keep it." I remember thinking that I was being very helpful by offering Russell this nugget of spiritual wisdom. I can't imagine what he must have been thinking, being confronted by some kid.

Like I said, though, Russell was kind. He responded kindly. Perhaps his kindness is what disarmed me. He didn't argue with me, but he didn't accept my viewpoint. Somehow he affirmed me and my beliefs without budging an inch on his own convictions.

As a result, I was inclined to affirm Russell. I probably couldn't have found the words to say this then—the fact that I was trying to correct his theology on our first meeting is evidence enough that I was a spiritual infant—but on an emotional level, I couldn't dismiss someone who had demonstrated such a high level of spiritual maturity. His unwillingness to fight with me won me over almost immediately.

Which meant that I now had something to think about. After all, if Russell was right, then I was wrong.

I started reading the Bible with a new unanswered question in mind: if all Scripture is inspired and all Scripture is useful (2 Timothy 3:16), and if the things that were written by Moses and the ancient prophets were written for our benefit (Romans 15:4), then how could Jesus simply toss aside the Law, the Pentateuch, the keystone and foundation of the entire Old Testament?

I mean, I know, Jesus fulfilled the Law. But how can it just be gone? Just like that? After being the definition of holiness and goodness for fifteen hundred years?

Now it wasn't just Jesus that made no sense. My theology of the Old Testament made no sense either. I was making real progress.

Messianic

This new question continued to color my study of the Bible. In time, I became obsessed with it. I knew that I was missing some critical information about the role of the Old Testament.

This was a surprise to me, because as a dispensationalist, I already believed that the Old Testament and the Jewish people were important. I can still remember when, long before my crisis of faith, I had been introduced to the teachings of a Messianic (Jesus-believing) Jew named Zola Levitt.

According to Zola, the timing of Jesus' crucifixion was predicted to the very day thousands of years in advance by the institution of the Passover festival in Exodus 12 and Leviticus 23. I can still remember when I was first exposed to this idea on one of Zola's VHS tapes (it was a long time ago). When I first heard him detail the connections between Jesus' death and the Jewish liturgical calendar, I was awestruck. Why had I never learned this before?

When I met Russell, I realized that there was even more to the story. Jesus did more than just fulfill the Passover through the timing of his crucifixion. He actually celebrated Passover and the rest of the Jewish festivals. He made them part of his religious life. But what did that mean for me as a disciple? Was I supposed to do that stuff too?

I didn't even know where to start looking for answers to these kinds of questions.

As it turns out, Zola Levitt was not the only Messianic Jew with a teaching ministry. But while it should have been clear to me that Messianic Judaism would have answers to some of my pressing questions, I didn't really know that it existed on any kind of broader scale. It would be years before I discovered what an incredible untapped resource Messianic Judaism represented. In the meantime, I continued to drift.

Michigan

When my mom retired, our whole family moved north. I settled only half an hour from where I live today, in a region of southern Michigan renowned for nothing but its seemingly limitless farm fields. A few big box stores, a couple of factories, and a quiet downtown formed the center of what was otherwise a completely agrarian community.

The rural atmosphere was a change from the busy Chesapeake Bay area. Nothing ever happened—and when it did happen, it took its time.

I finished my degree. The recession made it difficult to find work. I was new in town and didn't have a lot of friends. All things considered, I had a lot of time to think and little else to do.

I attended a little country church in a nearby village that took all of thirty seconds to drive through—and it only took that long because the speed limit slowed traffic to a crawl. The pastor's preaching style was exegetical; he explained whole books of the Bible one verse at a time, a chapter a week. The degree I had just finished was in biblical studies, so I was primed and ready for in-depth sermons.

I had always attended smaller churches, but this one was probably the smallest I'd ever been in. It was downright *intimate*. Everyone knew everyone else, and each week during worship we had a time in which people felt comfortable sharing whatever was on their heart.

It was exciting to be part of something so alive, so vibrant, and so tightly knit.

The pastor at this particular country church was in the process of embracing a "Hebrew roots" approach to the Christian faith. He didn't use the term "Messianic Judaism," but what he was doing and teaching was kind of like Messianic Judaism—it was a blending of the Christian belief in Jesus with Jewish traditions and practices. So we celebrated Passover and Tabernacles and met on Saturday mornings instead of Sundays.

I knew that most Christians would have chastised me for "going back under the Law," just like I had chastised Russell the kosher media consultant. But I didn't feel that way. I felt like I was walking right in Jesus' footsteps—like I was on a path that would lead me to where I could finally make sense of life, faith, and the Bible.

I was excited to meet other people who seemed to be traveling down the same road I was on. I learned a lot at that little church and built some lasting friendships there.

Nothing lasts forever, though, and our little congregation eventually dissolved.

But while I was there I learned something valuable. Another piece of the puzzle—a key piece—slid into place.

Epiphany

By the time I finished my degree, I had spent years trying to reconcile the tension between my own personal picture of Jesus—the radical, super-holy, unpredictable mystic—and the way Christians lived and acted. Over and over again I had been disappointed with myself (and with everyone else) for not living up to what I thought a Jesus-like life should look like.

All that time, I still struggled with trying to understand Jesus. The picture in my head didn't seem to fit what I read in the Gospels, but I couldn't find any other picture that worked either.

What I hadn't realized yet was that I was missing a key piece of information, a historical detail that would eventually correct my picture of Jesus and set me on the right path.

I found this missing piece at a conference I attended while I was still going to the little country church in Michigan. A gifted speaker gave a hard-hitting lecture about little churches like ours that were trying to find ways to adopt some Jewish practices into their congregational lives. He made it very clear that the Old Testament Law, the Torah, couldn't be put into practice without reference to Jewish tradition.

I didn't agree with his lecture when I first heard it; in fact, I was mad. I didn't think anyone else should be able to tell me how to celebrate Passover, or what kind of tent I was supposed to build for the Feast of Tabernacles. Besides, Judaism was *weird*—traditional Jewish interpretation and practice didn't really make any sense to me. Jewish tradition was too rigid, too inflexible, and too hard to follow. On top of that, I was sure that Jesus had come to overthrow the Jewish way of life and to start something completely new.

I spent about three minutes after that lecture trying to convince the speaker that I was right and that he was wrong. I gave it my best shot. And I failed. In fact, he won me over.

I learned several things that day, but the one I'm getting at is this: When people who are not Jewish and have no connection to a Jewish community try to imitate Jewish customs, they end up just making stuff up. They find their own ways to celebrate holidays like Passover and Tabernacles; they make up rules about what kinds of clothes to wear and what kinds of things are okay to eat—they invent their own traditions.

To make this whole endeavor even more complicated, there is a lot of misinformation out there about Jews, Judaism, and the Torah. It's easy to spend an hour on the Internet and think you have learned some really meaningful "Jewish" tradition, when it's very possible that you have just found a website created by someone who has never even met a Jewish person and has no idea what they are talking about.

Every piece of Jewish religious practice—from the liturgical calendar to the practical outworking of the purity laws to the traditions surrounding the festival celebrations—all of it was hammered out through years of debate and discussion within the Jewish community. Our little congregation had no connection with this community, so when we tried to figure out how the Law of Moses would apply in the life of a local body of faith, we ended up needlessly arguing over details instead of learning from the beauty and depth of the Jewish traditions that Jesus would have embraced.

So our understanding of the Mosaic Law needs to be filtered through Jewish tradition.

But how does that change everything? How did it change my picture of Jesus?

After that conference, I began to reread the Scriptures to see if Jesus and his disciples really followed Jewish traditions. First slowly, then quickly, the evidence began to mount up. It soon became too great for me to ignore. A startling picture emerged from the New Testament, a picture that forever changed the way I read the Bible and lived out my faith, that connected and clarified many of the things I had learned up to this point, and that answered many of my unanswered questions.

It was simply this: Jesus is Jewish.

"All right," you might be saying, your patience slipping away. "Tell me you didn't lead me on for sixteen manuscript pages to tell me that Jesus was Jewish. I already knew that. *Everybody knows that.*"

First, there is a big difference between saying that Jesus *was* Jewish and saying that Jesus *is* Jewish, and I don't think most Christians have seriously thought through the ramifications of a present-tense Jewish Jesus.

Second, most of us couldn't define what it means to be Jewish today, much less what it meant to be Jewish two thousand years ago. We've got to understand Jewishness before we can make any sense of the sentence "Jesus is Jewish."

Understanding Jewishness isn't as easy as we might think. Judaism today is usually thought of as a religion, but there are Jews who don't practice Judaism—we might call them "ethnically" Jewish. So what does it mean to be a Jew? Is "Jew" a religious term? An ethnic term? A national term?

In Jesus' time, the answer was "yes." If you were Jewish, you practiced Judaism and you were part of the Jewish nation. Your parents were probably Jewish, too (although people of other nationalities could become Jewish by converting to Judaism and joining the Jewish nation).

There were some exceptions, and not all Jews agreed on every detail of how, exactly, the Jewish religion was supposed to be practiced. Even so, when I say that Jesus is Jewish, I mean that he is *really* Jewish. "Ethnically" Jewish, "nationally" Jewish, *and "religiously" Jewish.*

As a religious Jew, Jesus kept the commandments of the Law of Moses according to the generally accepted traditions of Judaism. Not only that, but as any good rabbi would, Jesus commanded his Jewish disciples to continue living traditional Jewish lives—and they did. In fact, for the first few years after Jesus' resurrection, Christianity was simply Messianic Judaism. Until Gentiles began to join the movement, there was no such thing as a believer in Jesus who didn't practice Judaism in an accepted, traditional, "Jewish" way.[1]

This simple idea changed my life. Not so much because it immediately changed the way I lived out my faith, but because I finally understood something about Jesus the man. Not something doctrinal or theological. A real thing about a real person. I suddenly had a mental picture of Jesus that made sense. Jesus was a Jewish rabbi who practiced Judaism. He didn't abolish the Law of Moses;

he didn't gut the Old Testament of its central, primary, defining revelation. Jesus actually affirmed and lived by the Law of Moses, and passed that way of life down to his Jewish followers.

I had no way of knowing this then, but before I ever realized that Jesus was a practicing Jew, this awareness had already taken the world of historical Jesus scholarship by storm. Later in life, when I started my graduate studies, I found that my new picture of Jesus was shared, at least to some degree, by dozens of university scholars, published authors, and experts[2]—and while some of them weren't believers, many were.

I didn't have the education of these scholars. For me the realization of Jesus' Jewishness came from Scripture passages that finally seemed to make sense in light of the new kernel of truth I had learned from that gifted speaker. One after another they fell into place. In Matthew 5:17–20 Jesus calls down a curse on anyone who transgresses the Law. Matthew 23:2–3 records a command from Jesus that his disciples should obey even the stringencies of the scribes and Pharisees who sat on the Sanhedrin, the highest human religious authority in Judaism at the time. Deuteronomy 13 warns against any prophet that counsels the people of Israel to abandon the Law—so could Jesus be such a prophet? Deuteronomy 17:8–13 states that all Jews must follow the legal rulings of the Jewish leadership—so could Jesus have overthrown those rulings and traditions?

Then there were the apostles. They headed up a church in Jerusalem that was, down to the last person, zealous for the Law of Moses (Acts 21:20). Even Paul, who wrote most of the Bible verses that we memorize about not having to obey the Law, continued to obey the Law (Acts 21:24).

These passages began to turn up everywhere as I continued to study. Even the songs that Jesus would have sung in the synagogue. Psalm 1. Psalm 19. Psalm 119. All of these Scriptures suddenly emerged, on rereading, with an incredible newness and clarity.

It would not be an overstatement to say that for me, at that time, the Bible came to life.

And Jesus came to life.

As a Jew.

Interlude

The first thing you notice is the oppressive heat as you find yourself in the middle of a street in a little village on a sunny hilltop.[3] You look around and see flat-roofed houses tightly packed together on both sides of the street. No power lines, no cars—have you been transported back in time? Or to a third-world country? Africa, perhaps? Arabia? Definitely somewhere hot.

You suddenly become aware of an eerie feeling that you'd had but couldn't place until now: you are completely alone. The town looks as if its residents have all been raptured. It's not a ghost town; in fact, it looks well-lived-in. And that's the eerie part. You get the feeling that everything is where it should be, and would be, in a town that had been bustling with activity only a short time before.

The smell—you finally notice it. The smell, you think, gives the town's secret away. It is not the smell of car exhaust and factory smog, but neither is it the smell of a lifeless ruin. It is the smell of people, animals, and prepared food. Not just wood and stone and dust, but leather and lanolin-drenched wool. An earthy smell, permeated with the essence of life.

There are definitely people here. Somewhere.

After some deliberation, you decide that standing still won't get you anywhere. Choosing the direction that seems to lead toward the more built-up side of town, you begin to walk toward the bright eastern sky on the main road out of the village. On your way you take note of several large, open cisterns full of clear water. You notice that the dry heat has made you thirsty, but you refrain from drinking.

Between houses you catch a glimpse of a broad valley, rich with grain, to the south. You stop to look. The view, at least what you can make of it, is breathtaking.

As you gaze, you gradually become aware of a sound behind you. You turn to the north side of the road and pinpoint the source; it's coming from one of the larger buildings. Maybe someone rich lives here? No—the building is too big, too ornate. And too public. From the entrance you hear something like—chanting? Singing?

Your curiosity is piqued; you haven't seen anyone else around, so you assume that everyone in town must be here in this building. You take your chances and duck inside. You don't expect air conditioning, but at this point you'd do anything to get out of the sun.

The stuffy, humid air inside the building isn't much cooler than the air outside, but the flagstone floor radiates a comforting chill. As your eyes adjust, you quickly notice that the little building is packed full of people, standing nearly shoulder-to-shoulder, and they are all facing you. One of them is singing—if you could call it that. It sounds more like the droning wail of the Muslim call to prayer that seems to have found its way into the soundtrack of every TV show and documentary you've ever seen about the Middle East.

The rest of the people are swaying meditatively or else engaged in their own private murmuring. As you look at what appear to be contestants in a "longest beard" contest, the blood drains from your face. You realize that you have just intruded on what must surely be a Muslim mosque during one of the Islamic hours of prayer. Carefully, trying to look natural, as if you belonged there, you edge away from the doorway, scoot along the wall, and try to blend in. The eyes of everyone in the room follow you as you do. Your heart is pounding.

The prayer leader continues to drone on as if he had not seen you enter. He is chanting in a language you don't recognize, presumably Arabic. From time to time, the whole congregation joins him in a jumble of voices. The sounds are chaotic and disorganized, nothing like the unified sound of a responsive reading. Some of the people are almost shouting.

The cacophony fades, and the prayer leader resumes his droning. He sways to its rhythm. Some of the worshipers appear to follow his lead, but others look as if they are engaged in their own reveries, muttering personal recitations. As you wonder about it all, the prayer leader comes to a pause, and everyone says a word that you recognize: "Amen." The leader keeps going. And stops. Again, "Amen." Your natural instinct is to want to say the word along with everyone else, even though you don't know what you would be affirming. You think it must be some kind of a sin for a Christian to pray to Allah.

You find a discreet place to stand near the back. As the prayers seem to conclude with a final "Amen," you look up and notice that with ceremonial reverence a scroll is being unrolled on a stand in the middle of the room. A Qur'an, perhaps? One of the men begins chanting aloud as he reads from it, again in the same unrecognizable language. His voice intones the strange-sounding slur of syllables to a patterned melody. His careful gaze never departs from the text. You crane your neck to get a better view.

His asymmetrical beard masks a suntanned face. Dark hair and eyes finish the picture of someone whom you think could be stopped at the airport for a "random" security check. You watch as he finishes reading, takes a seat, and begins speaking. Some of the other people in the room sit down too, on the floor and on benches along the walls, but most remain standing. You decide to stay on your feet—you still aren't sure you want to be here.

As you watch, you realize that the reader—now, apparently, the teacher—is explaining the part of the scroll that he just read. As he speaks, however, other men in the room are voicing their own interjections, responding to his questions, raising objections, and expressing affirmations. At some points several men are speaking at once, and a few of them express themselves with such passion that it reminds you of the potential danger around you. You remember that Muslim extremists sometimes concoct diabolical plots in their mosques. Could this teacher be an ancient terrorist?

The teacher waits for silence before continuing his talk. He seems passionate—not angry but not at all passive. He spits the words from his mouth with authority. Even though you cannot understand a word he says, you can tell from the reactions in the room that his words are provoking his listeners to serious thought. They seem delighted. As he speaks, your eye is drawn to a flash of blue thread, which you notice decorates the fringe of the corner of his cloak.

Suddenly something clicks in your memory, and you recall a Bible verse in which Jesus criticized the Pharisees for "lengthening the tassels of their garments." So that's where you are! It's not a mosque. It's a synagogue in ancient Israel. And the teacher is wearing the very same long, decorative tassels mentioned in the Gospels. He must be a ringleader of those hypocrites—a Pharisee, a teacher of the Law.

Your heart skips a beat as the realization hits you. Could Jesus be here? Could he be among the listeners? You try not to draw attention to yourself as you surreptitiously glance at each man in turn. You can't see everyone, but every man you *can* see has the same blue threads. What awful luck—you are in Jesus' very own backyard, but you're surrounded by Pharisees! You are pretty sure that the Pharisees had something to do with Jesus being crucified, and suddenly your discomfort returns. Perhaps they are plotting against him right in front of you!

You start to think about an escape plan. But suddenly the room goes quiet. The teacher is looking toward—you can't see what—but then as he calls out, a woman begins to walk toward him.

As she steps into the light, you see that her spine appears to be severely bent. She takes her time, using the small but practiced steps she has learned to take so as not to aggravate the pain in her back.

Is she in trouble? Perhaps she has violated synagogue etiquette. Now that you think about it, were women even allowed in synagogues? You can't remember. Didn't you once hear a sermon about how Jesus was the only Jewish man who talked to women in public?

The teacher, however, doesn't look stern or angry. As the afflicted woman approaches him, he places his hands on her. She immediately stands up straight.

You look back toward the teacher as blood rushes to your face.

You have just witnessed a healing performed by the Son of God and Savior of the world.

And you didn't even recognize him.

Shock

When I discovered that Jesus was a practicing Jew, I was shocked.

I shouldn't have been, but I was.

Of all people, a dispensationalist evangelical Christian with a four-year college degree in biblical studies should have known that Jesus is Jewish.

But I could have walked right past Jesus on the street without recognizing him. I would have been looking for a king, a prophet, a savior, a priest—but I never would have thought to look for a Jewish rabbi with tefillin on his forehead and tzitzit on his clothes.

Why?

Because my whole Christian life I had been so laser-focused on *what Jesus did for me* that I hardly ever learned a thing about *who Jesus is*. And I don't think I was alone. In my experience, most evangelical Christians are in the same predicament.

If you're a student of theology, you might object; you might reply that Christology, one of the most complex and important and well-studied branches of Christian theology, is all about *who Jesus is*.

But I came to realize that when we analyze Jesus as a theological puzzle piece or as a checklist of doctrinal statements, we are not studying *who* Jesus is. Rather, we are studying *what* he is. We study the hypostatic union, we study Homoousion, we study divinity and humanity—we study these abstract concepts as if they were all we needed to know about Jesus. But we don't study the personality of Jesus, the man, the Jew, the rabbi, the warm-hearted and fierce-tongued son of a carpenter.

My failure to study and know Jesus as a *person*—that was my stumbling block for the first two decades of my Christian life. The human element was missing from my picture of Jesus. That's why the Gospels didn't make sense to me. I was reading them in search of theology, but the Gospels offered something different: a story of a rabbi who changed the world. I was mining for theological ore in an endless vein of narrative gold. Searching for rough in the diamonds and coming up empty-handed.

When I met the Jewish Jesus, I saw my Savior for the first time—not just as an idea or as a theological concept or as a set of doctrines to be believed, but as a person to be loved and followed and cherished.

I believe that I was saved when I accepted Jesus the Son of God when I was four years old. But I don't feel like I *met* him until almost twenty years later, when I learned that he had revealed himself to the world as Yeshua, the rabbi from Nazareth.

Chameleon

I have seen a lot of artistic depictions of Jesus—paintings, drawings, statues, mosaics, stained glass windows. Hundreds of thousands of these works of art are enshrined in churches and homes all over the world, and they all look different. An eminent Messianic Jewish writer, Stuart Dauermann, once described some of the depictions he was familiar with:

> Examine the church's artistic and literary legacy and you
> will detect amnesia concerning the Jewishness of Yeshua.

Instead, the church embraces a generic Christ, the cosmic Savior, the Man for Others, a Metaphysical Hero, a Chameleon Redeemer who blends in perfectly wherever he is found. In its paintings, icons, weavings, drawings, and sculptures, the church in every culture makes Jesus over in its own image. You will find the Gentile Christ with the aquiline nose, the rugged white Anglo Saxon Marlboro Man Christ, African and Afro-American Christs, Asian Christs, often in Buddhist postures of meditative repose, Indian Christs looking more Guru than "Jewru," Swinburne's conquering pale Galilean, Mexican Christos twisting in crucified agony, and various designer Christs, tailored to fit each consumer culture.[4]

Overall, Christians seem to be pretty comfortable with the idea that we can imagine Jesus however we want. Why can't we have a Caucasian Jesus or an African Jesus? In the end, who cares? If we are going to reach out to new cultures with the gospel, we have to show them something they can recognize, right? So if we can get people to believe in Jesus and adopt him into their cultural framework by tweaking him a little bit, or changing his skin color, so much the better.

Where does this belief come from? It reflects a deeper and more fundamental belief shared by most evangelical Christians: that it doesn't matter how we *conceive* of Jesus as long as we *believe* in Jesus. In other words, if we believe that Jesus is God and that he died for our sins and rose from the dead, then nothing else about him really matters. I mean, it all matters, but it doesn't *really* matter, because once you believe in Jesus, you're going to heaven, and everything else will be sorted out in the end.

This is a theological idea, and it is built on the even deeper belief that the only thing that matters is eternal life, and the only way to get it is to have good Christology—to believe the right things about Jesus.

But if Jesus' followers are supposed to become more and more like him—"everyone when he is fully trained will be like his teacher" (Luke 6:40)—then doesn't it matter what Jesus was like when he walked the hills of Galilee? Doesn't it matter a lot? Isn't a Jesus-like life the target we are all aiming for?

I think it is. But then what if we don't see the target? What if we don't see Jesus the way he really is? What if we have some other idea in our heads instead? Won't our journey, our path of discipleship, take us in the wrong direction? Won't we miss what we are aiming for?

I'm not talking about the fact that we all miss the mark because we all make mistakes. This isn't a conversation about how we are all sinners saved by grace. Of course we are all sinners saved by grace. But after we are saved by grace, we're supposed to get better. We're supposed to get closer and closer to a Jesus-like life. Whatever you want to call it—*imago Christi*, spiritual formation, sanctification—we are trying to be like Jesus. That's our target, the mark we're aiming for. That's *discipleship*. And what I'm suggesting is that even after we accept God's remedy for our sin, we can still fail to hit that target, not because of any natural tendency toward sin, but because we couldn't be bothered to find out where the target is to begin with. We can fail to grow into Christ's image simply because we can't see that image—we can't see what we are trying to become.

Most of us have some kind of picture of Jesus in our heads. As his followers, we are trying to become like that picture. But if that picture isn't clear, or if it isn't complete, then somehow we have to fill in the details. In my case, I began to believe that becoming a Christian meant becoming a radical and unpredictable agent of change, and becoming so holy that "normal" life held no appeal for me—because that's the kind of person I thought Jesus was.

I looked for this level of holiness, radicalism, mysticism, and unpredictability in other believers and in myself and I couldn't find it. That's why I grew disillusioned and cynical at Bible college. But I couldn't really find this Jesus in the Gospels either; and without an accurate picture of Jesus, I had no idea how to follow him. I became completely stuck in my walk of faith.

In the end, this "stuckness" was a blessing in disguise. It caused me to doubt that I was right about everything. It caused me to start reconsidering my assumptions. It helped me to let go of my own personal Jesus. It opened the way for me to see that Jesus is Jewish and that this changes everything for his followers.

Now that I had a picture of Jesus that made sense, and that seemed to help the Gospels make sense—in fact, more sense than they had ever made before—I decided it was time to straighten myself out. To get unstuck.

Change

Theology is like a tapestry, a finely woven cloth—like the one on the cover of this book. If one thread is pulled, the entire picture begins to change. If the tapestry is perfectly crafted, pulling threads will distort the image, throwing it out of balance or erasing key details. But if a thread is out of line, pulling it back into place will restore the picture that the artist originally intended to create.

When I finally realized that Jesus and his disciples were practicing Jews and that the worldwide religion we now call Christianity began as an expression of Judaism, I knew that I had some threads to pull. I was pretty sure I knew which ones to start with; at least, I was on the right track. The next step was to delve deeper, to study more, to revisit the Scriptures armed with a clearer picture of Jesus, and to begin making sense of it all.

I opened my Bible like an excited kid who had just learned to read. I bought books about the Bible and about Judaism, as many as I could afford, and I read them all. I wanted to know what it meant that Jesus was Jewish—how it affected my life, my faith, my walk. I wanted to know what else I had missed. So I read any scholar I could find who wrote about the historical Jesus.

I began studying at a theological seminary. I was preparing for the pastorate, but I also had an ulterior motive—to learn as much about the Jewish Jesus as I could. So I read the material the seminary assigned to me—books on preaching and spiritual growth and pastoring and church administration—but I also read the critics, the skeptics, and most of all, the scholars who believed that Jesus was a practicing Jew, and that this should mean something for his followers today.

When it comes to matters of faith, not all Christians are convinced of the value of academic literature—commentaries, journals, and other scholarly monographs about Jesus and the Bible. I wasn't convinced either, at first; I had grown up being taught that the Bible was all I needed in order to believe the right things and to live the right way. But I learned two things during my first week in seminary. First, all students of theology think they understand the Bible, but they all interpret it differently (and they can't all be right). Second, it didn't matter how I personally understood or interpreted the Bible; all that mattered was what I could prove.

I can still remember my first class, in which the professor told us that if our opinions were not supported by scholarly commentaries or other academic works, then our opinions were not worth considering. At all.

I learned quickly that it was not enough for me to cite a few Bible verses in defense of my positions. I needed to find scholars who looked at those verses the same way I did. People who had tried and tested their theories and written down their findings. People whose ideas had been analyzed and criticized and refined over many years. People with credibility.

Having to prove my beliefs to my professors didn't discourage me. I just studied harder. I read the arguments of scholars from many different backgrounds—Jewish scholars and Christian scholars, Protestants and Catholics and Orthodox, believers and nonbelievers. I didn't have the patience for interlibrary loans; when I saw a book I thought I needed, I bought it. Most of the books I ended up adding to my library weren't even required for my classes, but they opened the world of the New Testament to me in ways I never could have imagined.

Before long I could explain in precise academic terms why I believed that Jesus was a practicing Jew—and I could cite a dozen highly regarded scholars who saw the same Jesus I did.

Proof

Just a moment ago I mentioned that many Christians don't see much value in academic literature—at least, not when it comes to matters of faith. This is partly because so many university scholars have rejected the basic doctrines of Christianity. In fact, the generation of scholars that first said "Hey, look, Jesus was a Jewish guy" also rejected Jesus' divinity, his miracles, and his resurrection. So it's not hard to see why many educated evangelical Christians are generally not too excited about the quest for the historical Jesus—the efforts of university scholars who have tried to find out more about what Jesus, the person, was like.

Now that I am so firmly convinced that Jesus is Jewish, and that we must understand him in his Jewishness in order for us to begin to make sense of the rest of the Bible, I can see that it was important for these scholars to upset the status quo. When the quest for the historical Jesus began, back in the seventeenth century, the church's interpretation of the New Testament was off kilter. At that point in history, Christians assigned no real significance to Jesus' Jewish identity aside from the fact that he had to be Jewish to be the Messiah. In fact, the theologians of the church taught that Jesus came to overturn the Law of Moses and to do away with the Jewish way of life. This traditional Jesus didn't look anything like the Jewish rabbi of the Gospels, so it was only a matter of time before someone pointed out that the church had gotten a few things wrong.

At my conservative Southern Baptist seminary, though, these critical scholars were viewed with some degree of contempt—or at the very least, suspicion—because they had rejected the supernatural aspects of the Gospel stories. None of the professors ever came out and said it, but it wasn't hard to tell how deeply these feelings were held. Reimarus, Strauss, Renan, Schweitzer—these liberal scholars had overturned the traditional Christian faith and left nothing but an empty religion, devoid of the supernatural, devoid of life and power.

To me, the writings of the first historical Jesus scholars represented a double-edged sword. I couldn't believe, as they did, that Jesus was only a man. But at the same time, these scholars hit on an important truth that I couldn't ignore: whatever one might believe, the Jesus we read about in the Gospels was a Jewish man whose life and ministry must be understood in a Jewish context.

I had a problem, however, when it came to explaining myself to my Christian friends. It was hard to prove that Jesus was a practicing Jewish rabbi from the Bible alone. There is no verse that states outright, "By the way, Jesus was a practicing Jew; you should really know that if you want to understand everything else in this story."

We see the Jewish Jesus in the Gospels only when we understand their context—when we understand the world in which Jesus lived and taught. We have to be able to put ourselves in that world if we really want to understand what Jesus was saying. We have to be able to hear Jesus in the same way that someone who lived at that time, in that place, would have heard him. We have to have the same kind of common ground with Jesus that his original audience had.

Anyone who has ever taken English Literature should know how badly we need context in order to understand books from other cultures and time periods. When a high-school English Lit class reads one of Shakespeare's famous plays for the first time, do the students immediately laugh at all of the Bard's jokes? Do they understand his historical references, his allusions to other works of literature, his political satire, or his social commentary? Most students don't—at least, not right away. The teacher has to point these things out. He has to help his students understand what it was like to live in Shakespeare's time. He has to teach them about Shakespeare's *context*—the history and culture of Elizabethan England—before they can begin to appreciate the richness and depth of Shakespeare's drama.

Without context, we can read Shakespeare all day long and still never see the Bard's true genius. We will almost always miss the real significance of what Shakespeare was trying to say. We will be stuck trying to understand the surface-level stories and convoluted plots, and Shakespeare's deeper message will go right over our heads.

It's the same with trying to understand the Gospels—in fact, Jesus' first-century Jewish culture is even more foreign to us than Shakespeare's sixteenth-century English culture.

So while we might think Shakespeare is hard to understand, the truth is that the Gospels are even harder.

But like many hard things, studying Jesus' context is worth the effort. Imagine being able to hear Jesus' words with the same ears as one of the twelve disciples. Imagine being able to see Jesus' actions through first-century Jewish eyes, and to understand what significance they would have had to the people who surrounded him at that time and in that place. Imagine having an intuitive grasp of the Gospel stories, so that you could just sit down and read them without having to constantly wonder what Jesus is talking about, and why.

The closer we come to understanding Jesus' world, the closer we will come to this level of understanding. But, just as with Shakespearean drama, learning Jesus' context is easier said than done.

How do we know what Jesus' world looked like? How do we know how first-century Jews, the people Jesus spent his life with, would have understood Jesus' words and actions?

Context

How can we reconstruct the world Jesus lived in, a world long dead and buried under the dust of ages? Is it even possible?

The answer is "yes"—sort of. We can never know everything there is to know about the past. But we are living in an exciting time. Thanks to the efforts of thousands of researchers and scholars, today we have unprecedented access to Jesus' context. We have more information about Jesus' time, language, and culture than almost every generation of Christians that has come before us.

This information has come to us in several different ways: through archaeology, through the study of other Jewish writings from around Jesus' time, and through new ways of looking at the Bible. These three major disciplines, or areas of study, have slowly built on each other and reinforced each other over the course of the past few centuries. As a result, today we have a wide palette of colors with which to paint a fresh and accurate picture of first-century rural Galilee, Jesus' home and the base of his teaching ministry.

These disciplines are complex, and the documentation they produce—books, journal articles, dissertations, and conference papers—are often dry, technical, and difficult to understand. However, I know a lot of other believers who have taken the time to study this material, and they have all found great enjoyment and fulfillment in becoming, in essence, amateur archaeologists, historians, and sociologists.

The first area of study we are going to look at, archaeology, has had a massive impact on how we see and study the Bible. Archaeologists have excavated the ruins of Cana, Capernaum, Chorazin, and many other villages that Jesus lived in and traveled through. These ruins have taught us things about Jesus' culture that we never would have known otherwise. This pool of information grows all the time; every time we dig something up, we learn a little more.

Here I will just give one example of how archaeological discoveries have given us an important clue to Jesus' context: archaeologists have found evidence that supports the idea that first-century rural Galilean Jews—Jesus' people—were devoutly observant Jews. In fact, they didn't just observe the letter of the Law of Moses. They even embraced some of the traditions of the Pharisees.

We know from the Gospels that the Pharisees were tremendously concerned with ritual purity, an idea that is hard for American Christians to connect with because we have nothing like it in our culture. Ritual impurity can't be seen or smelled or sensed in any way, but many materials can "catch" impurity and spread it to other things and to other people. If a cup made out of pottery becomes ritually impure, it has to be broken and cannot be used, because it can transmit ritual impurity to whatever is placed in the cup—and according to the rabbis' interpretation of the Old Testament law, if you're Jewish, you don't want to be drinking ritually impure stuff.[5]

Stone vessels, however, don't transmit ritual impurity. Even if a stone cup once touched something ritually impure, whatever is poured into it later on does not automatically become ritually impure.

As archaeologists have excavated the ruins of the Galilean villages in which Jesus spent so much of his life, they have found in every case that the first-century Jews who lived in these villages made heavy use of stone vessels: cups, bowls, basins, and lids.[6] These items were so common that probably everyone had access to them. With stone bowls and cups in every house in Galilee, it is not hard to believe that Galilean Jews were doing their best to stay ritually pure.[7]

The study of ancient Jewish texts is a second discipline that has shed light on the world Jesus lived in. Devout Jews in and around the time of Jesus wrote many other books besides those included in the Bible. While I do not believe that these books were all inspired by God, they do tell us what Jews of ancient times thought about different ideas, what was important to them, and what their religious and spiritual lives looked like.[8]

In an example that relates directly to the stone vessels unearthed in Galilee, an ancient Jewish text called the Tosefta relates that in the years prior to Jesus' birth, "purity broke out in Israel."[9] In other words, more people than ever before became concerned about the laws of ritual purity and began to follow them more strictly.

When this text is considered along with the archaeological evidence mentioned above—the stone vessels—it becomes even clearer that the Pharisees weren't the only Jews concerned with ritual purity. Ordinary Jews were also very careful to keep themselves ritually pure.[10]

Whether Jesus was strictly observant of these laws or not, we now have some context: while Jesus walked the earth, every Jew in the towns and villages of rural Galilee probably observed the purity laws to some extent.

How does this help us understand Jesus? Knowing what we know about ritual purity in Galilee, it is safe to assume that Jesus probably obeyed the purity laws.

How do we know this? Because as an esteemed teacher, called "rabbi" throughout the Gospels not only by his disciples but also by those who didn't know him that well (John 3:2), it is almost certain that Jesus would have been known for keeping these laws—otherwise, how could he have had any credibility with his fellow Jews? Who would have listened to him? Would you listen to a pastor who did not seem to care about important Christian rules, like "don't cheat on your wife"?

Finally, new ways of looking at the Bible have helped us to see more of the context of Jesus' life and ministry. Let's take social-scientific criticism as an example. While it sounds like (and is) a very specialized field of study, social-scientific criticism is not that difficult to understand in principle. A scholar using this method of study will learn as much as he can about the social groups of Jesus' time (for example, Jews and Gentiles), what they thought of each other, how they interacted with each other, and so forth. With this background, he will have a better understanding of why the books of the Bible were written and how they would have been understood by the social group they were being written for.

Okay, maybe this discipline *is* pretty difficult to understand. An example of its usefulness might be better. After learning that ritual purity was very important to the Jewish people in Jesus' time, we might wonder why the laws of ritual purity are not mentioned very often in the New Testament, and are not found in the lists of commandments in Paul's epistles. Social-scientific criticism gives us one possible reason: these laws do not appear in most of the New Testament because most of the New Testament was written to

Gentiles, and according to the traditional Jewish interpretation of the Law of Moses, the laws of ritual purity do not apply to Gentiles.

Sola

As I learned more and more about archaeology, ancient Jewish literature, and academic Bible study methods, I began to understand why my own personal Jesus had been so different from the Jesus who actually walked the earth two thousand years ago.

I had been painting a portrait, but I had only half the colors I needed.

The Gospels cannot be fully understood by themselves. I know I'll ruffle some feathers by writing that, but it's true. The Gospels simply don't give us all the information we need in order to understand them—at least, to understand them as well as Jesus' original audience understood him. Just like you had to learn to read English before you could read this book, so we have to learn about the time and the culture and the language of the Gospels before we can fully understand them.

Many of Jesus' words, phrases, sayings, and parables can be properly defined and understood only within his first-century Jewish context; outside that context, they can be completely misinterpreted. The Gospel reader without this contextual information is left to his own devices. But our devices—context clues, dictionaries, and the other tools we learned to use when we first began to read—don't always help us cross the barriers of language and culture and time that stand between us and Jesus.

Commentaries and other Bible study helps are useful, but they can also take us in the wrong direction. Many commentators just don't take Jesus' Jewishness very seriously. Things are getting better; more recent commentaries generally do a better job of using Jewish literature and recent archaeology to understand and explain Jesus' context. But these commentaries are expensive, and they tend to be written in a dry and difficult-to-understand academic style.[11]

Even some lexicons and dictionaries, books that attempt to explain the original meanings of the Greek and Hebrew words behind the text of the Bible, can fall short in this area. Some were written before relevant archaeological evidence was unearthed and are simply out of date.[12] Others reflect a theological bias on the part of the translator.[13]

Most people who read the Bible don't dig down to this level of complexity. They are content to believe in the doctrines of their denomination, to ask their pastor for guidance, and to read books like this one that attempt to make all of these things easier to understand. But new archaeological discoveries, new insights into the biblical text, and new information from other ancient Jewish texts—all of these things are published in journals and books that most people don't have access to. All of that information takes time to filter down to seminaries, pastors, and popular Christian authors. With few exceptions, people change slowly, and organizations (seminaries, churches, and publishing ministries) change even more slowly.

So while a few popular Christian authors—N.T. Wright, for example—have made use of some of the newest scholarship on Jesus, most pastors, seminaries, and churches don't even have the Jewish Jesus on their radar.

The tide is turning, though, and I was lucky—I was given a leg up. As a seminarian, I had volumes of articles at my fingertips through academic databases; I could get around the outrageous subscription fees that keep scholarly journals out of the hands of most Bible readers. I was taught how to read and interpret dense and difficult academic writing. I had a growing library of scholarly books.

With every new book and every new study, I believed more and more strongly that Jesus lived the life of a pious, observant Jew, and that he had handed this way of life down to his disciples. While many scholars saw a different Jesus, I simply didn't find their arguments as convincing as those of scholars who saw Jesus as a Torah-observant Jewish rabbi with Torah-observant Jewish followers.[14]

Eventually, I became confident enough in my beliefs that I wanted to start applying what I was learning to my own life. What did my new discoveries mean for me? How would they change the way I lived out my faith?

I set out to learn more about what it was like to be Jewish in first-century Galilee. Before I jumped to any conclusions about how Jesus' own religious life should affect my own spiritual walk, I wanted more details.

I wanted to complete my mental picture of Jesus so that when I asked the question "What would Jesus do?" I would be able to find the right answer. I would be able to become a better disciple.

Part 2

The Jewish Jesus: A Portrait

.

The Carpenter's Son

Is not this the carpenter's son? Is not his mother called Mary? And are not his brothers James and Joseph and Simon and Judas?

— Matthew 13:55

You may be familiar with the story of Jesus' homecoming. After preaching to great crowds of people one day, Jesus sat down with his disciples for some small-group time. I imagine Peter, John, and the rest were in high spirits as they heard Jesus explain his parables in more detail. Their movement was growing. Their rabbi was inspiring. From a pastoral standpoint Jesus certainly had nothing to complain about. Sure, he had made some enemies, but as a pastor, I have found that preaching the gospel is a pretty surefire way to make enemies. No less a man than Charles Stanley was once punched in the face by one of his own deacons. So all things considered, by today's standards I would say that Jesus was doing pretty well.

Then Jesus went back to his hometown, to Nazareth, and gave a lesson in the synagogue there—he was the "guest preacher" that week.

Imagine that one of your childhood friends became a famous TV preacher. Then one day you see a flyer posted in your church—your friend is coming back to give the message this Sunday. Wouldn't you be excited? Wouldn't you mark your calendar?

I would think that Jesus' old friends, the ones he had played stickball (or maybe dreidel) with as a child, would have been happy to see him again, would have been excited that he was doing great things for the kingdom, and would have been ecstatic to see him give a lesson in their little synagogue.

But their response to Jesus' message was horrible. "We know this guy," the people said. "He's the carpenter's son. There's nothing special about him."

Our instinctive reaction is to think, *How could anyone say that about Jesus?*

Good question.

I grew up hearing this answer: the people in Jesus' hometown were just dullards. They had no faith because they were spiritually blind. They couldn't see Jesus' heavenly greatness because they were too concerned with earthly things.

But this explanation had never made that much sense to me. Why would Jesus go back to Nazareth and try to teach people who had no spiritual potential? Didn't he have better things to do?

In my studies I found out that my doubts were justified. I learned that the Jews of Jesus' time—at least, a good number of them—actually had *loads* of spiritual potential. They were devout. They had faith. They knew their Bibles. They were waiting for the Messiah to come. They were on the lookout for Jesus—they just didn't know yet that *this was him*.

So I had to consider another possibility. Maybe Jesus came off as a regular kind of guy.

Maybe, growing up, Jesus wasn't that different from your average Jew.

I mean, think about the other ways in which God has revealed himself. Take the Bible, for example.[15] As Christians, we believe that the Bible is divinely inspired. It is the only book on the planet that Christians believe God actually moved people to write, and word for word it is exactly what God planned for us to have. It is God's revealed Word. It is perfect.

But the Bible doesn't look supernatural. It's made of paper like any other book. Look at it all day long. Put it under a microscope. No hidden messages—nothing secret, nothing magical.

The Bible doesn't glow; it doesn't hum with supernatural energy. It's a very normal-looking book—how else could so many people have read it and still not believe it?

Jesus, as incredible as he was, evidently didn't strike his family or his neighbors as being especially amazing. Like the Bible, he was perfect; he was full of wonderful, incredible messages directly from God; but on the outside, he seemed—at least in some sense—like a normal person.

Well, a normal Jew, anyway.

But what was it like to be a normal Jew in Jesus' time?

Judea

Jesus lived in a Roman province called Judea. Before it was called Judea it had been known as the land of Israel, and before that, as the promised land of Canaan. It was called "promised" because God had promised it to his people; Israel was the land that God had given to Abraham, the father of the Jewish nation. It was the land in which the Jewish people had lived out most of their history—the land to which Moses had led the Israelites after the ten plagues and the parting of the Red Sea, and the land over which kings like David and Solomon had reigned in splendor.

But in Jesus' day Israel had been reduced to a shadow of her former glory. She had been conquered by the evil, godless empire of Rome. The Jewish people lived in subjugation to their Roman overlords, hoping for rescue yet fearing the inevitable crackdown that would come if anyone stepped out of line.[16] Crucified Jews were nearly always on display outside Jerusalem's gates, a constant and visible reminder of Roman oppression.[17]

The last hope of the Jewish people was an ancient prophecy of a coming king from a long-forgotten bloodline who would restore the old monarchy, take his rightful place on the ancestral throne, and—wow, this is starting to sound like *Lord of the Rings*.

But as hopeless as their situation seemed to be, the Jewish people had a lot going for them on the spiritual level. God had entrusted them with the only kind of Bible that existed at the time— the *Tanach*, which we call the Old Testament, a collection of inspired laws, writings, and prophecies. The first and most important part of the Old Testament was the Law of Moses, which contained the 613 commandments that God had given to Moses on Mount Sinai. (You can find that story in Exodus 19 and the following chapters.)

On top of that, hundreds of years of legal rulings and arguments had given birth to a very large and comprehensive set of traditions, today called the oral law (though it has since been written down).

The Jewish law, written and oral, enveloped every aspect of life. No question of religious observance—how to obey God properly in any given situation—went without an answer for long. In fact, more often than not, multiple answers were offered. Different schools, headed by different teachers (rabbis), had different interpretations of the Law. All agreed, though, that the Law (in Hebrew, the Torah) was valid. It was the final authority as to how all Jews everywhere were supposed to live.[18]

The Jewish people considered the Torah to be so important that they began teaching it to children at age five—starting with Leviticus, if you can believe it. Leviticus. The book of sacrifices, priestly requirements, ritual purity, and leprosy. The book that keeps most Christians from reading through the entire Bible, because when they get to Leviticus, all of a sudden the Bible gets *boring*.

Religious Education Then and Now

	Modern Christian Education	*Jesus' Jewish Education*[19]
Age 5	Kindergarten—Simple Bible stories like David and Goliath and Jesus' birth; basic manners	The stories and laws of the Old Testament, beginning in Leviticus
Age 10	Fifth grade—More complex stories like the life of Jesus, Paul's missionary journeys, and the Exodus; expected to have personal faith in Jesus	The oral laws of the Jewish people, hundreds of years of accumulated tradition
Age 13	Eighth grade—Confirmation in some denominations (if not earlier); basic church teaching, character development, analyzing and applying Old Testament stories	Began to be held legally responsible for observing all the Law's commandments as they were traditionally interpreted (*bar mitzvah*)
Age 15	Tenth grade—Doctrines like justification, sanctification, the Trinity, etc.; resisting peer pressure, remaining sexually pure	Jesus probably began to learn and practice his trade (carpentry) at this age

The Gospels don't give us very much specific information about Jesus' childhood. The Gospel writers just didn't consider it to be that important. However, in the early chapters of the Gospel of Luke, we catch a glimpse of this period of Jesus' life:

> Now his parents went to Jerusalem every year at the Feast of the Passover. And when he was twelve years old, they went up according to custom. And when the feast was ended, as they were returning, the boy Jesus stayed behind in Jerusalem. His parents did not know it, but supposing him to be in the group they went a day's journey, but then they began to search for him among their relatives and acquaintances, and when they did not find him, they returned to Jerusalem, searching for him. After three days they found him in the temple, sitting among the teachers, listening to them and asking them questions. And all who heard him were amazed at his understanding and his answers. (Luke 2:41–47)

We can see from this passage that Jesus' family observed the Jewish custom of celebrating Passover in Jerusalem every year. But we also learn something even more intriguing: Jesus was able to hold his own, at twelve, with the teachers of the Torah and of Jewish tradition. He must have shown great promise as a student.

I think we miss the significance of this passage if we forget that Jesus is a human being. We assume that he did well in his studies because he had a God-level IQ.

But I don't think Jesus "cheated" as a kid, using supernatural knowledge to pass his tests. The Apostle Paul wrote in Philippians 2 that Jesus didn't use his God-ness to his own advantage; instead, he humbled himself and lived as a regular human being. He would have had to learn to walk, talk, read, and write like everyone else: "Jesus increased in wisdom and in stature and in favor with God and man" (Luke 2:52). Jesus would have had no room to "increase," or grow, if he had started at the top, already knowing everything.

It can hardly be a coincidence that the one story we have from Jesus' youth is about his growing knowledge of the traditions and laws of Judaism. Although Jesus was an outstanding student, his dedication to Torah study would have been completely normal for any Jewish boy in Galilee. Along with all the other boys in his village, Jesus' entire life, from childhood on, would have been completely shaped by obedience to the Law of Moses.[20]

Jesus was a bright student, but he came from a poor family in a poor village. Financial constraints probably kept him from being able to continue his formal religious education past his early teens.[21] But until then, just as almost every child in our culture goes to school every day, Jesus learned the Torah—his "Bible"—every day.

Unlike most of us, Jesus grew up in a culture in which obedience to God was a defining aspect of life at all levels of society. Think of it almost like growing up Amish—daily life was highly regulated by tradition and religion. Also like the Amish, the Jewish community had ways of reinforcing the boundaries between insiders and outsiders. While some Jewish people had begun to abandon their ancient ways, in rural Galilee every Jewish boy would have grown up learning the difference between righteousness and sin, clean and unclean, "good" Jews—scribes, Pharisees, teachers of the Law, and everyone else who obeyed the Law of Moses—and "bad" Jews. Traitorous tax collectors. Corrupt Herodians. Jews who didn't really live the way a Jewish person was supposed to.

Jesus grew up knowing that if he broke the laws of the Torah, he could be brought before a rabbinic court, called a *beit din*. Like the Apostle Paul, who was repeatedly flogged by synagogue leaders, Jesus was under the authority of the Jewish religious judicial system. In first-century Galilee, obedience to God's law would have been the norm, the accepted way of life. Straying from this path would have invited punishment and isolation from the rest of society.

We should not be surprised, then, to find that Jesus is not the only person in the New Testament to be described as obedient, as blameless, as fulfilling all the Law's requirements. Similar statements are made about Paul (Philippians 3:6), Zechariah, and Elizabeth (Luke 1:6).

Backwards

Words cannot tell how confused I was when I first began to learn these things. The Pharisees were widely considered to be the good guys? The Jews actually obeyed all those commandments?

And God himself was in on it? He really expected the Jewish people to obey the Torah? I had always thought that the Law was too hard for anyone to follow.

I think that all this information was strange, was new to me, because I had learned Jesus backwards. I didn't start at the beginning with the little Jewish boy from Nazareth. Instead, I learned the last week of Jesus' life first—Jesus died for my sins and rose again—and never went back to seriously consider the rest of his story.

Actually, you know, most of us learn the whole Bible that way. Every Christian knows about the death and resurrection of Jesus, but most of us know next to nothing about the Jewish people, the promise to Abraham, the giving of the Law, the building of the Temple, and all the other things that led up to Jesus.

It's kind of like catching the end of a movie you've never seen before.

Imagine that you've never seen *Star Wars*. I mean the first *Star Wars*—the one that started it all, the movie that made sci-fi cool again. (If you've actually never seen *Star Wars*, this will be easy to imagine—but my analogy here might be hard to understand!)

Now imagine that some of your friends are watching *Star Wars* together, and you, late for the party, walk into the room just in time to catch the last few minutes. Your friends would rejoice at seeing a heroic Luke Skywalker blow up the evil empire's Death Star, but since you hadn't seen the rest of the movie, you wouldn't understand the significance of that final climactic battle. You would just see some guys in little spaceships blowing up a big spaceship. You might even find yourself feeling a little sorry for the thirty million or so people who got up that morning, ate breakfast, went to work, checked their e-mail, charged up the evil super-laser, and then were unexpectedly vaporized.

The entire story of *Star Wars* leads up to that single moment at which Luke fires the missiles and the Death Star explodes, but that moment needs the rest of the story in order to make sense. We feel happy when the Death Star explodes because of all the things that happened earlier in the movie. We root for the rebels because we know that the empire is evil; we've watched it do horrible things. We root for Luke because we've seen that he is a good person who is trying to help others, despite being down on his luck.

To really understand the end of a movie, we need context—we need to know the rest of the story. But when I read the Gospels as a young believer, I didn't have any context—I didn't have the whole story. I just had little pieces of it. As a result, I ended up following someone I didn't even really know. By the time I went back to study the Gospels in an attempt get to know Jesus better, I had made so many assumptions about Jesus that I couldn't make sense of his life and ministry.

Now don't get me wrong—I still believe that the resurrection of Jesus Christ is the keystone of the entire Christian faith. Everything hinges on that one critical moment. If Jesus hadn't come back from the dead, there would be no Christianity. We learn about the resurrection first because that miraculous event, attested to by multiple eyewitnesses, leads us to want to learn and study the rest of the Bible.

But for almost two thousand years, the church has done a poor job at that last part—at going back and studying the rest. In fact, starting in the second century, the early church began to downplay the rest of the story. As the apostles became a distant memory, later generations of church fathers didn't see why Jesus' Jewishness mattered. They didn't understand how the Jewish people fit into God's plan. Ultimately, most Christians simply forgot that Jesus was Jewish—or if they knew that he was Jewish, they weren't able to explain what that meant, or why it was important.

If the Bible were a movie, we would have rewound and played back the final scene over and over without bothering to go back and watch the whole story—the story of God's relationship with the Jewish people.

What happened as a result? The answer is uglier than any of us would ever want to admit. Most Christians know that Christianity was illegal under Roman law, and that Christians were heavily persecuted in the second and third centuries. But most of us forget that almost as soon as Christianity went mainstream, Christians became the persecutors. Church history is littered with examples of Christian oppression of Jewish people. In the late medieval period, we literally forced Jews to choose conversion to Christianity or death. In some places, if we suspected converted Jews of holding on to Jewish traditions—remember, these traditions helped shape and define Jesus' entire life—we dragged them from their homes into torture chambers and stole everything they owned.

I know I am getting myself into hot water by using the term "we." Someone is thinking, "I didn't have any part of that—it was a long time ago." Or even, "That wasn't me—I'm a Protestant, and those were Roman Catholics." But no matter which denomination or expression of Christianity we call home, our heritage includes mistakes, and some of those mistakes were violent, and a lot of that violence was directed toward the Jewish people. We may not embrace that heritage, but without it we wouldn't be what we are today.

Remember that the Apostle Paul described the church, the body of Christ, as one organism with many parts (1 Corinthians 12). When one part fails, it affects all of us. When the church, the institutional church, makes a mistake, we all own a part of that mistake. When one part of the body is sick, the whole body suffers.

If you're still not convinced, then at least try to look at the church from a Jewish point of view. Over and over throughout history, the institutional church has persecuted the Jewish people. It is absurd to think that the Jewish people do not remember these acts of violence. But who will repair the church's reputation? The people who committed these atrocities are long gone. *We* are the church now. If we think that this burden is not ours to bear, then we are thinking too small, and too selfishly. This responsibility is ours alone. No one but us can fix what previous generations have broken.

We can't fully make up for the mistakes of our past. We can't erase the black marks on our heritage. But there are some things we can do—and should do. And one of these things is to remember that God wrote a bigger story than the one we often tell. In part of that story, God started a relationship with the Jewish people. Along the way, he invented the Jewish way of life; he invented Judaism when he gave the Torah to the Jewish people.

God seemed to think that the Jewish people would be able to follow the laws he gave them, and he clearly asked them to give it their best effort. At the end of the Torah, after all the laws and instructions were given, Moses laid it out pretty plainly:

> I call heaven and earth to witness against you today, that
> I have set before you life and death, blessing and curse.

Therefore choose life, that you and your offspring may live, loving the LORD your God, obeying his voice and holding fast to him, for he is your life and length of days, that you may dwell in the land that the LORD swore to your fathers, to Abraham, to Isaac, and to Jacob, to give them. (Deuteronomy 30:19–20)

Jesus, and many other Jewish people in his time, took this choice seriously. They chose life. They obeyed God. They kept the Law.

So why did Jesus argue with the Pharisees so much? And why did his people reject him? We'll get to that. Learning the context doesn't mean that we forget the story. Starting the movie at the beginning doesn't keep us from watching the end.

But for now, know that Jesus lived a fully Jewish life, and spent his first thirty years learning the Torah and building farm equipment out of wood.[22]

Like a normal Jew.

Son of Man

Jesus said to him, "Foxes have holes, and birds
of the air have nests, but the Son of Man has
nowhere to lay his head."

— *Matthew 8:20*

"**J**esus," I want to ask as I read through the Gospels, "why do you keep talking in the third person?"

"It's weird," I add. "I'm going to have a hard time introducing you to my friends."

I think that Jesus' peculiar way of referring to himself was one of the reasons I had a hard time getting to know him. The way Jesus talks in the Gospels makes it hard to imagine him as a regular sort of person, someone you could really sit down and have a conversation with.

"The Son of Man has authority on earth to forgive sins" (Luke 5:24).

"The Son of Man came eating and drinking" (Matthew 11:19).

Somehow I just can't imagine Jesus being a lot of fun at parties, even though the Gospels record that he went to quite a few of them.[23] But isn't that the way we so often picture Jesus? Stoic, unyielding, mystical, detached?

I think we have a tendency to chalk these kinds of things up to Jesus' divine nature. We come to Jesus expecting something weird, something foreign. "Jesus is God, so of course he's going to talk and act a little differently."

But when we shrug our shoulders and say, "Jesus is just weird," it keeps us from asking any more questions. And if we don't ask, we won't get answers. If we don't dig any deeper, we miss the chance to learn something.

If we don't take the time to find out why Jesus refers to himself as the Son of Man, then this simple phrase actually becomes a barrier between us and Jesus, a wall that keeps us from understanding what he is trying to tell us. It makes Jesus inaccessible; it makes it hard for us to explain who he is and what he is like to other people.

In the last chapter we talked about how Jesus spent his entire childhood studying the Old Testament. His whole life was built on the foundation of the Torah and the Prophets. So if we're going to look for some idea as to where Jesus would have picked up such a strange turn of phrase, the Old Testament is a natural place to start.

Ezekiel

A quick search through the Old Testament for the term "son of man" reveals that it's not a very common phrase, but when it is used, it means nothing more than "a person." Big revelation there—a son of man is a person. It's a poetic way to refer to a human being.

However, there is one book in the Old Testament in which "son of man" is used pretty frequently. It is used by God himself, and he used it to refer to a prophet named Ezekiel. Over and over. In fact, the term "son of man" appears in the book of Ezekiel about ninety-four times, more than in all the rest of the books of the Bible combined.

Prophets were weird. Jonah got eaten by a fish. Elijah was taken up into heaven in a tornado. But Ezekiel was probably the weirdest prophet of all. He didn't want to be; it wasn't his fault. God just kept giving him weirder and weirder things to do.

God asked Ezekiel to build a little model of Jerusalem to act out its coming destruction. He asked him to lie on his side for over a year. He asked him to shave his head and act out a little drama with the hair. He asked him to bake nasty bread over a poop-fueled fire. All the while God kept calling him "son of man."

To put it in perspective, if someone came into your church and announced that God had told him to cook nasty bread over a poop-fueled fire to teach everyone a lesson about the economy, it wouldn't be long before the police, the fire department, the health department, and the local psych ward got involved. (I'm almost sure you wouldn't invite him into your small group.)

There's another unique thing about Ezekiel that most people skip over. It's his strange vision of God's chariot, which is recorded in the first few chapters of his book. Out of all the Old Testament prophets, Ezekiel is the only one who wrote down a detailed eyewitness account of God's *ride*, and it was a life-changing experience for him.

God's "chariot," or *merkava*, is apparently made of huge, incredibly scary creatures. Ezekiel described some of these creatures as *chayot*. Still today in Hebrew the word *chayot* can refer to a certain kind of angel, but these aren't the chubby little guys on the ceiling of the Sistine Chapel. Here is how Ezekiel describes them:

> As I looked, behold, a stormy wind came out of the north, and a great cloud, with brightness around it, and fire flashing forth continually, and in the midst of the fire, as it were gleaming metal. And from the midst of it came the likeness of four living creatures. And this was their appearance: they had a human likeness, but each had four faces, and each of them had four wings. Their legs were straight, and the soles of their feet were like the sole of a calf's foot. And they sparkled like burnished bronze. Under their wings on their four sides they had human hands. And the four had their faces and their wings thus: their wings touched one another. Each one of them went straight forward, without turning as they went. As for the likeness of their faces, each had a human face. The four had the face of a lion on the right side, the four had the face of an ox on the left side, and the four had the face of an eagle. Such were their faces. And their wings were spread out above. Each creature had two wings, each of which touched the wing of another, while two covered their bodies. And each went straight forward. Wherever the spirit would go, they went, without turning as they went. As for the likeness of the living creatures, their appearance was like burning coals of fire, like the

appearance of torches moving to and fro among the living creatures. And the fire was bright, and out of the fire went forth lightning. And the living creatures darted to and fro, like the appearance of a flash of lightning. (Ezekiel 1:1–14)

So now you know why, when people ask, "God, why don't you just appear and show yourself in your full glory?" God rejects their invitation. He turns them down for the same reason you don't show horror movies to a little kid. If God appeared before us, we would be paralyzed with fear. Looking at the way God chose to reveal himself to the world—through the humble carpenter, Jesus—I think God wants to show us a gentler side of himself. For now, at least.

Anyway, most of us have never heard of these *chayot*—after all, they only appear in one place in the Bible. Right?

Maybe not.

Fasting

Remember when Jesus went out into the wilderness and fasted and was tempted by Satan for forty days?

Mark 1:12–13 records that event pretty briefly: "The Spirit immediately drove him out into the wilderness. And he was in the wilderness forty days, being tempted by Satan. And he was with the wild animals, and the angels were ministering to him."

The Gospel of Mark was originally written in Greek. The Greek word translated "wild animals" means, well, "wild animals." So even a Bible scholar reading Mark in the original Greek would think that Jesus went out into the desert, and there were lions there, and angels ministered to him. We're not really sure what Mark is getting at, though.

It's only two verses. Mark's pretty fast-paced. Matthew and Luke expand a lot more on this period of Jesus' life. So when we get to this section of Mark, we usually read right over it.

But Jesus probably didn't speak that much Greek. Peter, the source for Mark's gospel story, probably wasn't that proficient in Greek either. Jesus and Peter grew up speaking Aramaic or Hebrew, the languages of the Old Testament.

The word that was translated into Greek and then into English as "wild animals" was, in all probability, the Hebrew word *chayot*, which can be translated "living creatures," "beasts," or, the way Ezekiel used the word, something like "really scary-looking angels."

Understanding this, the translators of the Delitzsch Hebrew-English Gospels rendered Mark 1:12–13 this way: "Quickly, the spirit brought him out to the wilderness. He was there in the wilderness forty days, and the *satan* tested him, and he was with the *chayot*, and the angels attended to him."

Is it possible that instead of fending off lions, tigers, and bears, Jesus actually had a supernatural vision of God's chariot like the one recorded in Ezekiel?[24]

Perhaps that vision helped to shape Jesus' self-understanding. He would have perceived from his experience in the wilderness that he, like Ezekiel, was an appointed prophet, a man with an important message from God. Perhaps he felt some affinity with Ezekiel, who was also in the position of being a human being—a "son of man"—whose destiny was marked with cosmic significance.

Prophet

Most people think that prophets are people who can see the future. They can't. No one but God can see the future.

Prophets are people who receive revelations or messages from God. These messages are usually intended for other people, so the prophet is sent to deliver the message. Think of Jonah, who was supposed to go tell the Assyrians to turn from their wicked ways, or Jeremiah, who told his people that if they fought the Babylonians, they were going to lose. Many of God's messages are about the future; this is how prophets got their reputation for being able to predict the future.

Many Christians believe—because we hear it from the pulpit—that Jesus' message was the revelation of his person, his identity. We are taught that the only thing we need to take away from the Gospels is that Jesus is God, and that he died for our sins and rose again. But this isn't entirely true. Jesus' identity and atoning death are major parts of the story—eternal-life-or-death parts—but they aren't the whole story. The Gospel writers spent a lot of time and effort writing down Jesus' message because they thought that *it* was important too.

Jesus' message is more than just an explanation of his identity. He didn't teach the crowds just because he wanted them to believe that he was the Son of God. Rather, God had a message for the Jewish people, and Jesus was the one appointed to bring that message. Like so many prophets before him, Jesus faithfully delivered God's message to the Jewish people.

Each prophet recorded in the Bible was also given a set of consequences—things that would happen if the people God sent him to didn't listen to his message. Many prophets, in order to get people's attention, began with the consequences and moved on to the message. Most of the prophetic books of the Old Testament begin with woes, calamity, death, and other nasty things that are about to happen to the Jewish people. But read on, and every prophet had essentially the same message: change your ways, and these things won't happen. God will forgive you, and everything will be fine.

Prophets and Their Messages

Prophet	Message	Consequences if message is not accepted
Elijah	Repent of your sins and obey the Law of Moses (1 Kings 18:18).	Drought (1 Kings 17:1)
Jeremiah	Repent of your sins and obey the Law of Moses (Jeremiah 7:3, 23).	Destruction of Temple and land (Jeremiah 7:20)
Isaiah	Repent of your sins and obey the Law of Moses (Isaiah 1:16–17).	Death (Isaiah 1:20), poverty (Isaiah 3)
Ezekiel	Repent of your sins and obey the Law of Moses (Ezekiel 14:6).	Death, famine, wild animals, disease (Ezekiel 14:21)
Hosea	Repent of your sins and obey the Law of Moses (Hosea 6:1–3).	Famine, calamity, captivity, death (Hosea 8–9)
John the Baptist	Repent of your sins and obey the Law of Moses (Matthew 3:7–8).	Death (Matthew 3:10)

These are just a few examples. Look up the passages yourself and study them. Carry your search into the other books of prophecy as well. You will find that every Old Testament prophet had basically the same job: call God's people back to faithful obedience to the Law of Moses, the Torah. Even John the Baptist had this same basic message.

What about Jesus, though? Didn't he come with a brand-new message? He couldn't have just told people to obey the Torah. That would be a disaster—there are big sections of the Torah that Christians don't obey. If we're on the hook for the whole Mosaic Law, then all of us are in a lot of trouble.

Jesus' message was something different—a message of love, peace, and reconciliation, not a message of strict obedience to some ancient code of laws. Right?

Well, let's look through the Gospels and find the first sermon Jesus ever preached. Here it is—Matthew 4:17: "From that time Jesus began to preach, saying, 'Repent, for the kingdom of heaven is at hand.'"

When I was a young believer, I didn't know what this verse meant. It's a little embarrassing to admit that, since Matthew's wording here makes it pretty clear that this verse was the centerpiece of Jesus' whole teaching ministry. But I guess that's why I went to Bible college—to learn.

In my freshman-level New Testament class, the professor explained that verse to us this way: "repent" means "turn around" or "change"; and since the gospel message is "believe in Jesus," "repent" must mean "turn away from unbelief, change your mind about Jesus, and accept him as your personal Savior."

At the time I thought this was a great explanation. Looking back, I can see why. Instead of Jesus' message pricking my heart, causing me to change my ways and become a better person, it became nothing more than an affirmation that what I already believed was correct and that I was okay the way I was.

Was this really Jesus' intention? To promote nothing more than a change of mind, and not also a change in the way we act?

Repent

The Hebrew word for "repent" means literally to turn around and go the opposite direction. Like all the prophets before him, Jesus told people to repent—to stop what they were doing and to do something different. But what exactly were they supposed to turn away from, and what were they supposed to do instead?

The answer is in the next chapter of Matthew. Jesus says in Matthew 5:17 that he didn't come to abolish the Old Testament Law. He then repeats several of the commandments God had given through Moses, and—don't miss this—he *strengthens* them.

He takes the Law, which most Christians believe is *really hard* to follow, and makes it *even harder.*[25]

Let's walk through a few examples of this.

Matthew 5:21–22 states, "You have heard that it was said to those of old, 'You shall not murder; and whoever murders will be liable to judgment.' But I say to you that everyone who is angry with his brother will be liable to judgment; whoever insults his brother will be liable to the council; and whoever says, 'You fool!' will be liable to the hell of fire."

In essence, Jesus was saying, "I know that Moses told you not to kill each other. But you should really keep yourself from anger. That way you'll never want to kill anyone, and you'll be sure to obey God's commandment not to murder."

Here's another example. Matthew 5:27–28 reads, "You have heard that it was said, 'You shall not commit adultery.' But I say to you that everyone who looks at a woman with lustful intent has already committed adultery with her in his heart."

To use more modern vernacular: "Moses told you not to commit adultery. But the path that leads to adultery begins with lust. If you never start down that path, you'll never reach its end."

Matthew 5:33–37:

> Again you have heard that it was said to those of old, "You shall not swear falsely, but shall perform to the Lord what you have sworn." But I say to you, Do not take an oath at all, either by heaven, for it is the throne of God, or by the earth, for it is his footstool, or by Jerusalem, for it is the city of the great King. And do not take an oath by

your head, for you cannot make one hair white or black. Let what you say be simply "Yes" or "No"; anything more than this comes from evil.

Again, the essence of Jesus' message here: "Moses said not to break your vows. But if you don't make them, you won't break them. Just be consistent, trustworthy, and reliable, and you won't even need to make vows."

And so forth.

That's the essence of the Sermon on the Mount. In his teachings Jesus wasn't bringing people something completely new—a new code of ethics or a brand-new way to live. He was telling them how they could be absolutely sure of obedience to the law that God had already given his people—the Law of Moses. He raised the bar for daily living by putting safeguards in place to keep people far away from sin.

Some of Jesus' most famous statements actually came directly from the Law of Moses—statements such as "love the LORD your God with all your heart" (Deuteronomy 6:5) and "love your neighbor as yourself" (Leviticus 19:18).

So really, the "repent" part of Jesus' message wasn't any different than the message of the prophets before him. Like Isaiah, Jeremiah, Ezekiel, and the rest, Jesus preached, "Repent of your sins, and obey the Law of Moses." And like the rest of the prophets, Jesus told God's people—the Jewish people—what the consequences would be if they didn't listen to his message: the Temple would be destroyed (Matthew 24:2), and "great tribulation" would come upon Israel (Matthew 24:21).

The parable of the tenants (Matthew 21:33–46) illustrates this point. Jesus compares himself to the last in a long line of messengers from a vineyard's owner to his tenants, all bearing the same message.

This is not to say that Jesus is no different from the Old Testament prophets. He is different. But we get into trouble when we start to assume that Jesus was so different, so incredible in his identity as the Son of God, that this difference, this identity, is all that matters—and that his message is irrelevant.

Matthew, Mark, and Luke spent page after page recording Jesus' message—the message of repentance. Just like the Old Testament prophets, Jesus spent years preaching the message of repentance from sin and obedience to God's laws, and warning of the consequences if Israel failed to listen.

Jesus' message *does* matter. It matters so much that long before Jesus came to earth, God sent dozens of prophets to Israel with the same message: "Repent, or judgment will come. Obey the Law of Moses, the Torah. Keep my commandments."

This message is just as valid now as it was two thousand years ago. God still calls out to the Jewish people. Jesus' voice echoes through history, speaking to his people who have forgotten him.

"Repent; obey the Torah; keep the commandments."

Rabbi

There was a man of the Pharisees named
Nicodemus, a ruler of the Jews. This man came
to Jesus by night and said to him, "Rabbi, we
know that you are a teacher come from God, for
no one can do these signs that you do unless God
is with him."

— *John 3:1–2*

C hristians don't have rabbis. If you go to a church and ask to see
the rabbi, you'll probably get a funny look. People will tell you
that you have come to the wrong place. You don't go to church
and expect to see a rabbi there—rabbis are Jewish; they practice
and teach Judaism. That's a different religion.

Right?

Well, that is not entirely true. Christians have always had a rabbi.
His name is Rabbi Yeshua—Rabbi Jesus the Nazarene.

Like today's rabbis, Jesus taught the Torah and practiced Judaism. In Jesus' lifetime there was no such thing as Christianity. Jesus
didn't have any followers who weren't Jewish. He rarely even talked
with Gentiles. In fact, once when some Gentiles asked Andrew if
they could see Jesus, the Master tactfully refused to see them. While
Jesus didn't deny their request outright, the Greeks never got to see
the Rabbi from Nazareth (John 12:20–26).[26]

Jesus never went to Sunday school and never learned to say
the Lord's Prayer. He never made the sign of the cross or said the

Hail Mary. He didn't believe in *sola scriptura* or the Westminster Catechism. He was baptized, but not by a pastor—he was baptized by a Jewish prophet named John. He wasn't a member of a church, and he never sat in a pew.

Think about that. Jesus wasn't a Christian. He was a first-century practicing Jew.

In fact, Jesus was a devout Jew. He didn't just practice Judaism to the minimal standard of his society. He was outstanding. He was truly pious. He was a rabbi.[27]

When I say that Jesus was a rabbi, I mean that he was a teacher of the Torah and of the Jewish way of life. These rabbis set the bar for their communities; they were extremely serious about Judaism and worked hard to be holy and to obey God's commandments.

Rabbis in Jesus' day were not exactly the same as rabbis are today. They weren't like pastors. They didn't perform weddings or anything like that. They weren't ordained or accredited or licensed either.[28]

Rabbis were simply experts in the Law of Moses; many of them were blue-collar working people who spent all their free time studying. "Anyone could become an expert" if they spent enough time reading and learning.[29] They didn't need a degree from a university (there weren't any).

So let's say you were a Jew living in Jesus' time, and you were listening to the Old Testament being read in the synagogue, and you heard Leviticus 23:22:

> When you reap the harvest of your land, you shall not
> reap your field right up to its edge, nor shall you gather
> the gleanings after your harvest. You shall leave them for
> the poor and for the sojourner: I am the LORD your God.

If after hearing that passage you had a question about *exactly how much* of your barley harvest you were supposed to leave in your field for the poor, you would probably ask a rabbi.

Incidentally, the rabbi may have said something like, "There is no prescribed measurement, but traditionally, we recommend that farmers leave one sixtieth of their barley out in the field for the poor to collect and eat."[30]

Jesus was a rabbi, an expert in the Law of Moses. He would have been able to answer people's questions about how to obey God. He might have answered a bit differently than other rabbis of his time, but not because he didn't know the laws and traditions. He simply had different priorities.

Pharisees

Because the entire life of a Jewish person was based on the Torah, rabbis were highly respected. Many rabbis were from a certain party called the Pharisees; one ancient historian recorded that the Pharisees were popular and that people liked them.[31]

From what we know about the Pharisees, I think most Christians would actually like them too. Most Pharisees were regular working people who took the Bible (at that time, the Old Testament) really seriously. It's nice to have someone in your neighborhood who is just like you, someone who works for a living, who knows the Bible really well. You can go to that kind of person and get real-life answers to questions about God and how you are supposed to live. Pastors love this kind of person too—lay experts can help a lot with counseling and mentoring in a local church.

I know that this doesn't mesh well with what most of us have heard about the Pharisees. Most Christians think that "Pharisee" means "hypocrite." But who would join a group called "The Hypocrites?" Who would want to have anything to do with them? Common sense tells us that there must be something more to the idea of being a Pharisee.

Even Jesus, who seemed to disagree with the Pharisees all the time, didn't find *all* of their teachings objectionable. In fact, Matthew 23:2–3 records that he commanded his own disciples to follow the teachings of the Pharisees, as they were adopted and enforced by the Sanhedrin. Apparently, however, not all Pharisees lived the way they taught other people to live. They didn't follow their own advice. They were, in the fullest sense of the word, hypocrites. Jesus' harshest criticism, his most scathing rebuke, was reserved for these false-faced pretenders (see the rest of Matthew 23).[32] There is no reason to believe, though, that all Pharisees were this way. Otherwise it would be hard to imagine why they were so popular.

If you think about it, today's Christians aren't so different. All Christians believe that we should help the poor, visit the sick, and live lives of humble holiness centered on Jesus. It's easy to go to church on Sunday and pretend to be a person who does these things. It's easy to talk about God a lot and how dedicated you are to serving him. But many of us are no different from the Pharisees Jesus criticized. What we're saying is good, but we don't live up to our own standard. We talk the talk without walking the walk.

It's important to remember that when Jesus criticized the Pharisees, he wasn't criticizing them because of their Jewishness, because of their strict observance of the Torah, or even primarily because of their teachings (though he did rebuke them for some of their interpretations). He was criticizing them for the same reason he would criticize many Christians today: for not being honest about how well we are living up to the standard God set for us.

Disciples

Most Bible teachers today don't travel around with a band of disciples, stopping at scenic locations to dispense Bible knowledge. Because this teaching method is so weird, it is easy for us to assume that Jesus was an innovator, that Jesus invented the idea of making disciples. However, by the time of Jesus, discipleship was a well-established practice in Judaism.[33] Having disciples was completely normal for a rabbi of that time.

The relationship between a rabbi and his disciples was structured.[34] It was formal, sort of like the relationship between a lawyer and his client. If a man were to go to a random lawyer and confess that he had committed a crime, the lawyer could turn him in to the police. But once you have hired a lawyer, a formal relationship is established. Within that relationship, normal rules don't apply.

A person can tell his lawyer anything—he can confess to all kinds of heinous behavior—and the lawyer isn't allowed to tell anyone. We call this rule attorney-client privilege. But it exists only within the bounds of that formal relationship, a relationship that exists only once someone has hired a lawyer. And it applies only between those two people.

The disciple-rabbi relationship was formal, too. Within that relationship, special rules applied. Disciples and rabbis each had clear roles, clear expectations, and clear responsibilities. When someone signed up to become a disciple, he knew what he was getting into—and it wasn't easy.

Disciples are students, but they're more than students. They don't learn the same way we learn from Sunday school teachers or college professors. Disciples in Jesus' time actually memorized the teachings of their rabbi word for word. Think of the pages and pages of information we would all have to memorize in order to be fully trained disciples of Jesus!

But wait—there's more. In addition to learning from their rabbi, disciples imitated their rabbi—even in the small details of daily life. It's not hard to understand why; as an expert in the Torah, the rabbi was expected to do everything according to the laws and traditions of the Jewish people. If a disciple wanted to be as obedient as possible, he would just act like the rabbi.

Finally, disciples would raise up more disciples. The cycle continued, generation after generation, as the student completed his training, became the master, and made more disciples. Jesus stopped that cycle for his followers; we don't become masters, and we don't raise up our own disciples. All of us are disciples of one Master, Jesus (Matthew 23:8). But it is still our responsibility to make more disciples of Jesus—people who memorize his teachings and act the same way he acted (Matthew 28:19–20).

It is hard to be a disciple of Jesus today. We can't follow Jesus through the Galilee. We can't watch and imitate him. We can't hear his voice. We can't ask him questions.

But we do have the Gospels. Once we begin to get a handle on who Jesus is—a Jewish rabbi who operated within a Jewish context—his teachings and the stories about him begin to take on deeper meaning and greater significance. When we finally come to the point at which we understand Jesus, his words become immensely powerful. The life-changing power of Jesus' teachings cannot possibly be overestimated.

As Jesus himself taught, "Out of the abundance of the heart [a person's] mouth speaks" (Luke 6:45). Reading Jesus' teachings—once we are in a position to understand them—is like having direct access to his heart.

As a rabbi, Jesus had a lot to say. As his disciples, we need to learn those teachings by heart. As we hear and obey Jesus, our hearts cleave to his, and we become more like him. This is a key and foundational part of discipleship—and it's a part that we can't really do without developing our understanding of Jesus, his time, his culture, his religion, his life.

Curriculum

As a Jewish rabbi, Jesus was an expert in the Law of Moses, the Torah. He knew the ins and outs of the Torah, and he was familiar with the different schools of thought about how a Jewish person should obey God in the most appropriate way. In some Gospel stories we catch a glimpse of Jesus' encyclopedic knowledge of the Jewish traditions of his day.

Mark 7:10–13 is one such example. Jesus references a question that most of us have never had to ask: what can someone do if he has taken a vow to dedicate some of his wealth to God—specifically, the wealth that should have been used to care for his aging parents—and then changes his mind? Can he be released from his vow and help his parents, or is he stuck with his poor decision?[35]

For Jesus, the answer was a no-brainer. Helping one's parents is more important than a poorly-thought-out promise. But some Pharisees disagreed. They would hold such a person to his vow, and keep him from using that money to care for his parents. Jesus didn't try to hide his disappointment with them.

To Jesus, this particular interpretation reflected out-of-whack priorities. The Pharisees who held this opinion could technically say that they were teaching people to obey the Law of Moses—keeping one's vows is, after all, required by the Torah (Deuteronomy 23:21). But the way Jesus saw it, these particular Pharisees had actually neglected a more important law: "Honor your father and your mother" (Exodus 20:12).

As Jesus taught his disciples, day after day, they would have learned the right way to deal with these kinds of difficult situations. Jesus would have taught them which of the 613 commandments of the Torah were more important and which were less important. That way, when they ran into a situation in which two commandments conflicted, they would know which one took priority. His disciples probably knew the Law of Moses by heart and would have learned from Jesus how to be knowledgeable, pious Jews practicing Judaism.

After learning that Jesus and his disciples practiced Judaism, one of the books I went back to study first was Acts. As it turns out, Acts makes a lot more sense once we realize that we are reading about Jews practicing Judaism. The idea that Jesus taught his disciples to obey the Mosaic Law is seen on nearly every page of Acts once we understand what we should be looking for.

For example, Acts 4:1–22 records the story of Peter and John speaking before the Jewish leadership. The highly educated members of the Sanhedrin were "astonished" at the "boldness" of these country fishermen (Acts 4:13). Jesus gave his disciples a strong foundation in the traditions of Judaism, and they had no problem holding their own before Jews who'd had much more formal education. They could speak with confidence, knowing that they had learned everything they needed from Jesus.

But hidden underneath this whole passage is an even greater insight into the religious lives of the apostles. Notice that the Sanhedrin punished the apostles only because they were teaching about Jesus' resurrection from the dead, and not because they had broken Jewish law. How much easier would it have been to keep the apostles quiet if they had been breaking Jewish laws and traditions left and right? The apostles could have—and would have—been tried for those offenses instead.

That's how the legal system works; if the police want to arrest someone, they arrest him for whatever they can pin on him. They might not be able to prosecute him for the worst thing he did, but at least they are able to prove his guilt for the minor offense and get him locked away. The mobster Al Capone is a famous example of this principle at work. Despite his many violent crimes, Capone was eventually arrested for the relatively benign crime of tax evasion.

But when the apostles came before the Sanhedrin, they weren't charged with breaking any Jewish laws or traditions. They suffered only for their testimony of Jesus.

The Sanhedrin really wanted to nail the apostles. The power players didn't want to hear anything more about Jesus; that's why they had him killed to begin with. If they had been able to convict the apostles of some kind of crime against Jewish law, they would have pressed charges against them. But they didn't. For the apostles to have had such a clean "rap sheet," they must have been committed to keeping the Law according to generally accepted Jewish traditions.

Later on, in the last chapters of Acts, Paul suffered similar treatment; he had to be falsely accused of bringing a Gentile into the Holy Temple, a strictly forbidden act under Jewish religious law. If Paul had actually thrown off all the traditions of Judaism, the Jewish religious leadership would not have had to try to pin false accusations on him. They could have just jailed him for actually breaking Jewish religious law. But they couldn't—because he didn't.

So we can be confident that Jesus taught his disciples well, and that he covered all the bases when it came to Jewish observance.

Application

Jesus didn't just teach the words of the Law of Moses to his disciples. He taught them how to apply those words, just as pastors today teach their congregations how to apply the Bible to their lives.

Jesus' basic principle for interpreting and applying the Law is most obvious in the Sermon on the Mount (Matthew 5–7). As we saw in an earlier chapter, in the Sermon on the Mount Jesus repeatedly references commandments of Moses, but then teaches that just following the letter of the law isn't enough. Following the well-known rabbinic principle of "building a fence around the Torah,"[36] Jesus taught that people must be incredibly careful not to break God's commandments—so careful that they had to add extra safeguards to make sure that they stayed far away from sin.

I do the same thing with my young children. We heat our house with wood; it's cheap and renewable energy. All winter the wood stove is too hot to touch. Naturally we have a rule that the kids aren't allowed to touch the stove—not just in the winter when it's hot, but all year long. This rule is for their own protection. I don't want them to get into a habit of touching the stove in the summer when it's cool. They would be in for a nasty surprise when they went back to touch it in the winter when it's dangerously hot.

If my children break the rule in wintertime, the consequences aren't negotiable. The stove is hot—period. Touching the hot stove will lead to burned hands every time. Fire has no mercy. And while even children have to live with the consequences of their actions, as a parent, I still feel that I should protect my children from life-changing injuries.

So to make it less likely that my kids will have to take a trip to the hospital burn ward, I built a fence around my stove. It's possible that the little ones could pile up toys and boxes and climb over the fence, but at least that will give me time to catch them before they get to the real danger: the wood stove. In the same way, if we are careful to guard ourselves from negative feelings such as anger toward others, we will be less likely to hurt others with our words or actions. We might still get angry, but if we follow Jesus' teachings, we will be sensitive enough to realize that we must be extra careful how we handle that emotion.

Method

Jesus sometimes taught these things in simple, direct language. He was especially direct when he taught about obedience to the Torah and repentance from sin.

But Jesus had another major focus in his teaching ministry: the coming kingdom of God. The kingdom of God was going to be the end result of the repentance of the Jewish people. If they had obeyed Jesus' message, they would have been able to take part in the immediate restoration of the whole world. The kingdom of God would have been established on earth in a real, physical way. And that is a tough concept to wrap our heads around—it's hard to imagine a perfect world while we are still confronted with the day-to-day reality of a fallen, sinful planet.

There was another problem Jesus faced when he taught about the kingdom of God: a kingdom needs a king. Jesus understood that he was the Messiah, the one prophesied to take on that kingship. But in the first century, there were others who claimed Jesus' throne. The infamous Herod Agrippa spent his whole life chasing the title "King of the Jews." The Roman Emperor, Tiberius, enforced his own kingship with unsurpassed military force. So Jesus couldn't exactly run a get-out-the-vote campaign. He had to approach the subject sideways—he had to tell his fellow Jews that he was the promised king, but he had to do that without drawing too much attention to himself from the Herodians and Romans.

So sometimes, for sticky subjects like the kingdom of God, Jesus used stories—parables. His use of parables can be confusing to us for many reasons. For one, sometimes we miss his point because he was talking to a society that was predominantly agricultural. Like our great-great-grandparents, regular people in Jesus' time and culture spent most of their time working hard in fields. Their lives depended on it. If food didn't come at harvest time, no one ate.

Families and communities were different too. The system of government was different. Idioms and metaphors and word pictures were different. Even something as simple as an animal fable from Jesus' time might make no sense to us today. For example, while foxes in Western literature are crafty and shrewd, foxes in Jewish culture are animals who might have influence for a short time, but ultimately don't matter at all.[37] Think about how this might change your interpretation of Luke 13:32, which begins, "Go and tell that fox [Herod]…"

Because Jesus' world was so different from ours, his parables don't always make sense; this is one reason why some Bible readers think Jesus purposefully made his teachings hard to understand by cloaking deep mystical concepts in seemingly simple stories.[38] However, parables in Jesus' time were usually used to make things easier to understand. The stories he told were often designed to make his teaching accessible to day laborers, children, and others who did not have Jesus' aptitude for Torah study.

I'm not saying that Jesus never used a story to conceal a deeper truth; we know that he did. Certainly some of his stories were carefully worded to hide his true intentions from the Romans, while revealing them to his Jewish followers. On top of that, Jesus kept some things hidden from everyone, and a few teachings he reserved for his closest disciples. But while Jesus certainly didn't reveal everything clearly, we must be careful not to make things more mystical than they need to be. Much of what Jesus taught is clearer than it appears to be at first glance. Once we begin to understand his time and culture a little better, some traditionally mystical passages begin to lose their mystery. So when we see Jesus starting to tell a story in the Gospels, we should usually assume that he is trying to help us understand something, and not that he is hiding something from us, or passing down some esoteric or secret doctrine.[39]

It's almost time to move on, but as we paint the rest of the Jesus picture, let's keep in mind that Jesus' curriculum, the body of teaching he gave to his disciples, consisted of the laws and traditions of Judaism. He taught them to be pious Jews who obeyed the Torah as well as possible in all situations. Because the Torah was a direct revelation from God to Moses at Mount Sinai, people from all different backgrounds—not just Jews—have found many of Jesus' teachings to be intuitive, wonderful, and immediately relevant. (After all, many sayings of Jesus are so simple that they cross the barriers of time and culture with little difficulty. Think of the parable of the lost sheep.)

God is the God of everyone. So it is not surprising that the words of Jesus often resonate with all different kinds of people from all walks of life. But during his earthly ministry, Jesus was careful to restrict his teaching ministry to Jewish people, because Jews were the only ones who knew the Torah or were required to obey it, and because they were uniquely chosen and called by God to shine his light to the other nations of the world through obedience to that Law:

> See, I have taught you statutes and rules, as the LORD my God commanded me, that you should do them in the land that you are entering to take possession of it. Keep them and do them, for that will be your wisdom and your understanding in the sight of the peoples, who, when they hear all these statutes, will say, "Surely this great nation is a wise and understanding people." For what great nation is there that has a god so near to it as the LORD our God is to us, whenever we call upon him? And what great nation is there, that has statutes and rules so righteous as all this law that I set before you today? (Deuteronomy 4:5–8)

Excluded

On the preceding pages, I've given you a picture of Jesus that might be different from the one you are used to. Jesus was a Jewish rabbi who taught other Jews—not Gentiles. He had disciples just as every other rabbi did, and he taught them to obey the Old Testament Law. This picture of Jesus might make you uncomfortable.

If you grew up being taught, as I was, that we Christians are special, we are chosen, we are uniquely called, and the Jewish people are not, it can be genuinely upsetting to see the tables turned and to realize that the Jewish people are also special, chosen, and uniquely called.

If we grew up seeing Jesus through the lens of the first thing most of us learned about him—"He came to earth to die for *my* sins"—it can be genuinely upsetting to learn that Jesus rarely talked with Gentiles at all, and that he spent his entire ministry teaching Jewish people.

In fact, for those of us who aren't Jewish, most of the Bible reads like someone else's story—once we really start to understand it, at least. God called Abraham—not anyone else. The whole rest of the world is going to be blessed because of this calling, but the whole rest of the world was not called. Only Abraham was. The promise then passed by Ishmael and went to Isaac; it passed by Esau and went to Jacob. The promise was exclusive, not inclusive. No one else at that time got to be a part of it.

Paul harps on this point in Ephesians 2:12: "Remember that you were at that time separated from Christ, alienated from the commonwealth of Israel and strangers to the covenants of promise, having no hope and without God in the world." Separated, alienated, strangers. According to the Apostle Paul, that is what it means to be a Gentile.

But I promise that there is more to Jesus than what I have written here so far. His earthly ministry to the Jewish people is only part of the story. We are getting to the rest. But if we are going to encounter Jesus the way that he obviously wanted us to encounter him, the way he presented himself to the world, this is where we have to start.

The end of the story needs the beginning and the middle.

King

It was the third hour when they crucified him.
And the inscription of the charge against him
read, "The King of the Jews."

— Mark 15:25–26

When I was in college—a fundamental Baptist college—one of the hottest topics of discussion was whether or not we actually had to do what Jesus said.

You might think I'm kidding. I'm not. The college even brought in a guest speaker to try to straighten us out, to settle the debate between those of us who believed in "lordship salvation" and those who embraced "easy believism" (yes, they are silly terms—each one of these groups got its name from people on the opposite side of the argument).

These two terms might be foreign to you if you've never been around fundamental Baptists. But the ideas behind them are simple: Do we have to accept Jesus as Lord and actually pledge to obey him in order to be saved? Or can we just accept Jesus as Savior and be saved regardless of our intentions to obey?

Can we just believe in Jesus and be saved, or do we actually have to listen to him?

I can remember thinking that the debate was surreal, that it was totally disconnected from reality. I still think so. I know that a lot of my fundamentalist brothers who have spent long hours advocating one or the other of these ideas will probably think that I am trivializing all of their hard work. But honestly—how can a person have any inkling of who Jesus is, and categorically decide not to obey him?

I don't really get it. If we believe in Jesus, then we believe he is the King. The Lord. The Boss. *Our* Boss. There is no other option. Kingship is an integral part of his identity. The fact that some Christians have lost sight of that fact is evidence to me of how far we have come from a really biblical idea of who Jesus is. We have forgotten that there is no such thing as a Jesus who is not our king, a Jesus we don't have to obey. That's a Jesus we'll never find anywhere in the Bible—the one who came to save our souls but doesn't tell us what to do.

One of the first things we learn about Jesus in the Gospels is that he was destined to become the King—specifically, the King of the Jews. In Matthew 2:2, wise men from the east ask Herod, "Where is he who has been born King of the Jews?" I'm sure you have heard that line in a Christmas pageant delivered by the stammering, nervous lips of an eight-year-old kid with a plastic crown on his head (when I was eight, that was me).

But what do we do with that information? King of the Jews? Many of us don't even know any Jews. In the meantime, we are happy to acknowledge that Jesus is *our* king. And indeed, in Matthew 28:18 Jesus claims "all authority in heaven and on earth." So as it turns out, he *is* our king—whether we "accept" him or not.

But even as we sing "All Hail King Jesus," we often forget what that really means, because in the western world we've gotten rid of most of our kings. In Jesus' time, kings weren't elected, and no one could recall them. There were no votes or ballot boxes; people didn't get to choose—the king was the king.

Well, in a sense, there was a choice; people could choose not to obey the king. But the king was still the king, and he had the ability to make someone's life difficult—prison, fines, death—if that person decided not to do what he commanded.

The difference between democracy and monarchy is pretty well represented by a certain Monty Python sketch. Graham Campbell, playing a straight-faced King Arthur, is asked by a peasant to identify himself. When he responds that he is "king of the Britons," the peasant scoffs, "I didn't vote for you." Campbell pauses, incredulous, and says, "You don't vote for kings."

Jesus' kingdom is not a democracy or a representative republic. There was no Constitutional Convention. No one got to vote. God didn't ask the world if it wanted a king; he just gave us one. He gave Jesus authority over everyone. Those who accept his kingship willingly will be rewarded; those who don't—well, Jesus has the ability and authority to make their lives (and afterlives) difficult.

Boss

Imagine that you are a supervisor or a manager at a local business. You have an opening on your staff, and you want to hire someone from outside the organization. You advertise the position and because the economy is rough, you end up getting over a hundred applications. You narrow it down to seven people you want to interview.

After the interviews are done, you deliberate, you seek counsel, you do second and third interviews, and you narrow the pool further and further until one applicant—one in a hundred—is chosen. This applicant shines above the rest. His résumé is impeccable. He aced his interviews. He is amazing. You call him and offer him a job. He accepts.

The new employee arrives the next Monday for training. Due to his broad range of responsibility and the numerous regulations and processes his job entails, staff training takes an entire week. The following Monday he shows up for work. You put him at his desk. You show him how to dial out.

And that's it. You are proud of your choice; you have high hopes that your business will thrive due to the positive impact of this brilliant new person you have hired.

You come in the next day and see that he is already seated at his desk. You happen to catch a glimpse of what he is working on, and you see that he is reading books and researching ways to do his job better. You smile at his initiative and go about your work for the day.

The next day you arrive and notice that he is on the Internet, reading blogs and watching videos related to his job.

The next day he is logged onto the company website learning about the history of the company, its goals, and its projections for the future.

After a few weeks, you do a little digging and find that your new employee is simply not doing his job. He has taken no action toward meeting his deliverables. He has made no sales, sealed no deals, shipped no product.

He has learned a lot about what he should be doing—but he isn't doing any of it.

What kind of boss would you be if you took no action in this situation?

How would your other employees feel if you let this new employee continue to mess around all day?

Jesus used the example of an employer, or master, and his employees several times in his parables. The parable of the talents. The parable of the minas. The parable of the vineyard and the tenants. In each of these stories, God is pictured as an employer, and his people are pictured as his servants, his workers. Each time, the slackers—the workers who don't even try—get fired.

Actually, it's a little worse than that.

Sometimes the parable ends abruptly, and the lazy employees get thrown into "outer darkness" (Matthew 25:30). Why? I don't know, but I can guess. Maybe it's because there isn't a metaphor or allegory powerful enough to describe how God feels when his people completely ignore his directions.

I have to think that if Jesus were here, really here, we would take his orders more seriously. Can you imagine Jesus sitting on the throne in Jerusalem? The ancient monarchy of David renewed, the king's palace rebuilt, its splendor restored? Jesus' presence here on earth visible and tangible? Everyone in the world able to see him and hear his voice? If this were the case, wouldn't we be more scrupulous, more careful in our words and actions?

Would we argue about lordship salvation and easy believism?

When we decide to follow Jesus, we decide that even though we can't see him, even though he is not physically here, we are going to be just as scrupulous, just as careful as if he were visibly sitting on his throne. We are going to obey Jesus as our king, even though we can't visit him in his palace or see him giving speeches on TV.

Even though we weren't there to follow him across the rolling hills of Galilee, or to hear him warn his disciples of the perils of being an unfaithful servant, as Jesus' disciples we have committed to live our lives in submission to his rule.

Nations

As Jesus' followers, it makes sense to think of Jesus as our king. But we must return to the question: why King of the Jews? What's so special about the Jews that Jesus, who has all authority in heaven and earth, is uniquely their king and not King of America or King of the Britons? After all, Jesus has many more American followers than Jewish followers. What does it mean to be King of the Jews? What's the significance of that term?

If you grew up in American evangelical Christianity, as I did, you might have a hard time with a God who is the God of a particular nationality. In America, everyone is equal in the eyes of the law—or at least, they're supposed to be—regardless of their country of origin. Evangelicals teach that everyone has to make a personal decision to follow Jesus, regardless of their religion or nationality. How can God play favorites? How can Jesus single out a specific nation to be "king" of—especially a nation that, for the most part, has rejected him?

But Jesus didn't live in post-civil-rights America. There was no such word as "racism" in his day; every nation had its own common ancestors, its own gods, its own land, and its own customs. There was no real "melting pot." If you were in someone else's country, you were a foreigner. For the most part, wherever people traveled, they retained their identity as citizens of their home country, as members of the extended families that built up nations.

In this way the Jews were no different. There were Romans, Greeks, Africans, and other foreigners in Judea at the time of Jesus, but they knew that they weren't really *home*. Rome's ever-expanding peace might have allowed many people to travel to different places, but people retained their ancestral identities and continued to worship their ancestral gods. Similarly, Jews lived all over the Roman Empire, but even in exile they continued to meet together as Jews and to worship the God of their ancestor Abraham.[40]

It was to this ancient world, a world before modern ideas of ethnicity and nationality and religion, that the God of all creation decided to make himself known as the God of the Jews. He could have chosen any nation, or all nations, but he chose to cultivate a unique, special relationship with the Jewish people. So Jesus, the one God sent to right all wrongs, came as a Jew, and one of his most important titles is "King of the Jews."

The throne of Israel belongs to Jesus by right, in part because he is from the bloodline of the ancient kings of Israel. For God's promise to David to be fulfilled (2 Samuel 7:16; 1 Kings 9:5; Jeremiah 33:17), one of David's descendants must eventually sit on the throne in Jerusalem—forever.

Because Jesus is King of the Jews, he is eligible to be the Messiah, the Anointed One who will bring an everlasting peace to the world—but we'll get to that in a later chapter.

Delegation

Because God chose Israel to be the unique vessel by which he would reveal himself to the world, Jesus didn't interact with Gentiles very much. His mission was to "the lost sheep of the house of Israel"—the Jewish people (Matthew 10:6, 15:24). So how do we know what Jesus wants from us if we're not Jews? What about us Gentiles?

Does Jesus want his Gentile followers to live Jewish lives, as defined by the traditional governing bodies of Judaism (Matthew 23:2–3)? He certainly placed this responsibility on his Jewish followers.

If this command applied directly to Jesus' Gentile followers, then we'd have to start living according to Jewish tradition. A strict interpretation of this passage would place us under the authority of the *Shulchan Aruch*, the currently recognized authoritative codification of Jewish law.

Before you start getting any ideas, I'll tell you right off that this isn't possible. There are too many complications, too many issues involved. A person simply has to be Jewish to live as a Jew. It's only possible to live a Jewish life when one is part of Jewish community, and Jewish communities don't let people in unless they're Jewish.

Somehow, though, we are supposed to know what it means to follow Jesus' instructions, despite the fact that his instructions were given in a Jewish context to Jews living under Jewish religious law. We need to figure out how to imitate Jesus even though we are not living the kind of life he lived—a Jewish life in a Jewish community.

Fortunately, Jesus knew that we were going to have these questions. In his wisdom, at the end of his ministry he took some final steps to make it easier for non-Jews to understand how to follow him. Just before he ascended into heaven, he gave his disciples a job: to teach all the nations (Gentiles) the things that Jesus had taught (Matthew 28:19–20). He gave his disciples the power to decide what we as Jesus' followers would be allowed to do and what we would be forbidden to do. This is the meaning behind Jesus' statement in Matthew 18:18: "Truly, I say to you, whatever you bind on earth shall be bound in heaven, and whatever you loose on earth shall be loosed in heaven."[41]

As a result, we have some clear and reliable sources that tell us exactly how Jesus' teachings are supposed to be interpreted and applied for non-Jews: the historical decisions of the apostles as recorded in Acts (particularly Acts 15) as well as the epistles of Paul, Peter, and John. (Hebrews, James, and Jude were probably written for a Jewish audience.)[42]

Furthermore, three of the four Gospels—Mark, Luke, and John—were probably written primarily with a Gentile audience in mind.[43] They tend to filter Jesus' teachings in a way that makes them applicable directly to Gentile believers.

Finally, an early second-century text called the *Didache* contains many traditions from the time of the apostles. This text is not in the Bible, but it is very ancient, and it is addressed directly to Gentile believers from the believing Jewish community—the apostles' community. In fact, the *Didache* is probably the only text we have from the time of the apostles that gives a comprehensive idea of what the apostles would have expected from non-Jewish believers; Paul's letters were not meant to be all-encompassing, as he wrote to address specific problems.[44]

Taken together, these texts give us a good idea of how the apostles, Jesus' appointed leaders, directed his Gentile followers to live. You are probably already familiar with many of the relevant passages:

Do you not know that the unrighteous will not inherit the kingdom of God? Do not be deceived: neither the sexually immoral, nor idolaters, nor adulterers, nor men who practice homosexuality, nor thieves, nor the greedy, nor drunkards, nor revilers, nor swindlers will inherit the kingdom of God. And such were some of you. But you were washed, you were sanctified, you were justified in the name of the Lord Jesus Christ and by the Spirit of our God. (1 Corinthians 6:9–11)

The works of the flesh are evident: sexual immorality, impurity, sensuality, idolatry, sorcery, enmity, strife, jealousy, fits of anger, rivalries, dissensions, divisions, envy, drunkenness, orgies, and things like these. I warn you, as I warned you before, that those who do such things will not inherit the kingdom of God. But the fruit of the Spirit is love, joy, peace, patience, kindness, goodness, faithfulness, gentleness, self-control; against such things there is no law. And those who belong to Christ Jesus have crucified the flesh with its passions and desires. (Galatians 5:19–24)

Therefore my judgment is that we should not trouble those of the Gentiles who turn to God, but should write to them to abstain from the things polluted by idols, and from sexual immorality, and from what has been strangled, and from blood. (Acts 15:19–20)

Let love be genuine. Abhor what is evil; hold fast to what is good. Love one another with brotherly affection. Outdo one another in showing honor. Do not be slothful in zeal, be fervent in spirit, serve the Lord. Rejoice in hope, be patient in tribulation, be constant in prayer. Contribute to the needs of the saints and seek to show hospitality. Bless those who persecute you; bless and do not curse them. Rejoice with those who rejoice, weep with those who weep. Live in harmony with one another. Do not be haughty, but associate with the lowly. Never be wise in your own sight. Repay no one evil for evil, but give thought to do what is honorable in the sight of all. If possible, so far as it depends on you, live peaceably with all. (Romans 12:9–18)

These passages, along with many others, define the responsibilities of the non-Jewish follower of Jesus. These are the things our king, Jesus, has commanded us to do through his servants, the apostles. As you can see, a life of discipleship isn't easy. In fact, the bar has been set pretty high. There is no shortage of commandments in the New Testament, and like the commandments of any other king, Jesus' rules are non-negotiable. Because of Jesus' kingship and authority, we are absolutely required to follow his teachings and obey his directions.

Unlike the commandments of other kings, however, Jesus' instructions for us come straight from the heart of God. Those of us who follow Jesus and love God should do everything in our power to obey these commandments—not just because we have to, but because we *want* to obey the one who saved us.

But even if we obey out of love and not out of a sense of obligation, we have to remember that obeying Jesus is still an obligation. Obedience isn't just for the especially devoted. It isn't a super-high plane of spirituality reserved for the ultra-pious mega-Christian. Obedience to the King is mandatory; it's for all of us, and if we're serious about our responsibility, we can do it—through Christ who strengthens us (Philippians 4:13).

Redeemer

Now when these things begin to take place,
straighten up and raise your heads, because
your redemption is drawing near.

— *Luke 21:28*

After Jesus died and rose again, he appeared to two of his disciples—not two of the Twelve; Jesus had many other disciples—who were leaving Jerusalem and going back home.

They had given up. Their hopes had been dashed. Not only was their Savior dead, but his body was gone, and the women were seeing crazy visions of angels.

These guys just needed a break. But Jesus decided to mess with them a little bit. He appeared next to them as they walked along, kept them from seeing who he was, and tried to get them to talk about what had happened. He claimed not to know anything about the recent crucifixion of Jesus the Nazarene.

One of the disciples explained the situation this way:

> Jesus of Nazareth, a man who was a prophet mighty in
> deed and word before God and all the people ... our chief
> priests and rulers delivered him up to be condemned to
> death, and crucified him. But we had hoped that he was
> the one to redeem Israel. (Luke 24:19–21)

We had hoped. We had thought that he was going to redeem Israel. But he didn't.

What's wrong with this picture?

Shouldn't this disciple have said, "Jesus just died to redeem us from sin and death, so I'm going to go home and throw a party"?

Instead of believing that Jesus had redeemed them through his death, the disciples thought that Jesus had failed to redeem Israel. How could they have mixed things up so badly?

It's hard for us to see the answer today, because "redemption" is one of those words we only ever hear in church. Unless we look it up in a dictionary, we can't really get an idea of what a word means if we never use it in regular conversation.

For example, if we drank from a bottle when we were little, we probably saw the bottle over and over again while hearing our caregiver say the word "bottle." Eventually it clicked that "bottle" was that thing that milk came from, and we eventually learned to ask for it by name.

But "redemption," like other theological words, isn't something we normally talk about outside of a religious context.

Perhaps because of this, the term "redemption" has developed two completely different uses in Judaism and Christianity. When Christians think of redemption, they think of the forgiveness of sins. Christ redeemed us by dying for our sins and removing the consequences of sin: death and separation from God. Jesus "bought" us with his blood.

In Judaism, on the other hand, redemption is defined as national deliverance from slavery or exile. The quintessential redemption of the Jewish people was the redemption from Egypt. I am sure that you have heard the story, or sung the song "Let my people go!"—or at least seen a movie about the exodus. Moses came to Egypt where the children of Israel were working as slaves. God used Moses and his brother Aaron to send ten increasingly severe plagues on the Egyptians until finally Pharaoh relented and let the Israelites go.

Soon after, however, Pharaoh changed his mind and chased the Israelites all the way to the Red Sea. The sea opened for the Israelites, and they passed through on dry ground. Then, when the Egyptian army tried to walk through the parted waters—*shloop!* The sea returned to normal, and all the bad guys drowned.

This redemption event is rehearsed every day in Jewish prayers all over the world. Every morning, as part of the prayer liturgy of Orthodox Judaism, hundreds of thousands of Jews recite the Song at the Sea, with which Moses and all the Israelites thanked God for redeeming them out of slavery in Egypt.

In Judaism, the redemption from Egypt is seen as the pattern for a great future redemption, called the *geulah* (pronounced "guh-oolah"). In the *geulah*, all the Jews who have been scattered all over the world will be gathered back to Israel in a state of blessing and peace under the great Messianic King. All God's promises to the Jewish people will finally be fulfilled, and the world will enter an unprecedented era of peace and prosperity: the Messianic Age.

Definitions

These two definitions of redemption—personal forgiveness of sin and national return from exile—are hard to reconcile. To make our task even more difficult, these two redemptions are directed at two different groups of people. Christians believe that only Christians are redeemed from their sins, while traditional Jews believe that the promise of return from exile applies uniquely to the Jewish people. What are we to do?

The obvious solution is to check out what the Bible has to say. While we don't have the space here to examine every use of the word "redemption" in the Bible, we can pick a few representative examples.

Predictably, the word "redeem" is used to describe the deliverance from Egypt (Exodus 6:6, 15:13)—score one for the Jewish side. Nothing about forgiveness of sins there.

But Romans 3:24 seems to use the word differently. Paul describes his audience as being "justified by his grace as a gift, through the redemption that is in Christ Jesus." This would seem to conform to the Christian usage. It doesn't seem to have anything to do with the Jewish national redemption; Paul was writing to Gentiles.[45]

Before we conclude that these two examples just represent a difference between the Old Testament and the New Testament, let's look at two more verses. One is Luke 24:21, discussed above, in which two disappointed disciples of Jesus lament to a "stranger" (Jesus himself, in disguise) that their hoped-for Messiah had died: "But we had hoped that he was the one to redeem Israel." These two disciples didn't think that Jesus had just died to redeem them from their sins. They thought that he had failed in his mission to end the exile.

And again, if you think that Jesus' disciples were just confused, Jesus himself uses the word "redeem" this way when he prophesied of his return in Luke 21:28: "Now when these things begin to take place, straighten up and raise your heads, because your redemption is drawing near." This future redemption must be the regathering of the people of Israel; a Christian is redeemed from sin—bought with Christ's blood—when he gives his life to Jesus. We don't have to wait until the second coming; Paul speaks of our redemption in the past tense (Galatians 3:13).

On the other hand, the Old Testament prophet Hosea describes God as redeeming his people from death (Hosea 13:14). This doesn't seem to refer to a national regathering. This sounds more like a final victory over sin and the grave.

So both ideas—national regathering from exile and the freedom from sin and its consequences—seem to be found in both the Old and New Testaments. It looks as if neither Jews nor Christians have a monopoly on the idea of redemption. Rather, Jews and Christians emphasize different uses of the word in the Scripture.

Slavery

The Bible has a lot of metaphors. Most of us learned in grade school that when we use metaphors, we call something what it isn't in order to make a point. We use metaphors all the time, and they make things easier for us to understand. But for a metaphor to work, we need to be familiar with the concept or object to which the original idea is being compared, and we also need to be aware that a figure of speech is in play—that the metaphor is not literal, but figurative.

For example, professional wrestler Dwayne Johnson goes by the ring name "The Rock." If a small child heard you call someone The Rock, he or she might imagine a person made of rock, a literal man of granite. When the child saw Dwayne in person, he or she would probably be confused, because Dwayne isn't a rock at all. He's a perfectly normal human being.

But to an adult, calling a wrestler The Rock isn't confusing, because everyone knows what it means. Dwayne is called The Rock because he is a tough guy. Like a rock, he can stand up to a lot of pressure and not break. The metaphor makes sense, even though on a strictly literal level, it isn't correct to call a person a rock.

The Bible's metaphors are sometimes just as easy to understand as the ones we use every day in English. For example, we have our own "Rock": Peter. His name, Petros, means "Rock" in Greek. His Aramaic name, Kefa (in some translations, Cephas), also means "Rock." Jesus gave him this name because Peter was going to be a key foundational person in the early church.

This is all very simple, and you may wonder why I'm going on and on about it. But some metaphors, especially metaphors from other cultures and languages, are not so obvious. We almost need to start from scratch if we want to understand them. We need to remember some principles of communication that we don't have to think about very often, since we follow them automatically when we use our native language.

We don't always expect the metaphors we encounter in the Bible. One of these metaphors is found in the word "redemption." Based on the way this word is used in the letters of Paul, Christians believe that the concept of redemption in the Bible means deliverance from sin and death. They don't understand the traditional Jewish definition of redemption as the return of the Jewish people from exile.

In reality, though, both uses are metaphors. The plain meaning of the word "redemption" is to buy freedom for a slave. The first time the Bible uses this idea as a metaphor, it refers to the "buying" of Israel out of the land of Egypt. The "price" of Israel's redemption was the slaughter of Egypt's firstborn. Israel to this day consecrates her firstborn sons to God in remembrance of the price of her freedom (Exodus 13:2, 15; Numbers 3:11–13).

Obviously, this is not a literal redemption. The whole payment scheme is different from what it would actually look like to buy a slave's freedom. But the term "redemption" is used metaphorically to describe how God set the Israelites free from slavery in Egypt.

According to the Apostle Paul, all of us are slaves—slaves to sin (Romans 6:15–23). The metaphor of slavery is used to describe how everyone seems to sin, whether or not they were really planning on it. The desire to do what is wrong seems to have a hold on us; even when we try to be perfect, we still fall into sin. We are, metaphorically, slaves to our own desire to do what is evil.

"The wages of sin is death" (Romans 6:23). So the long, weary trek of life, plagued by sin and resulting in death, can be metaphorically described as slavery. Like the mythical Sisyphus, who was forever rolling a boulder up a mountain only to see it roll back down again, we are trapped in never-ending servitude. We are slaves, forever working, with no end in sight except the depressing finality of death.

The Apostle Paul uses the metaphor of redemption to describe how Jesus bought our freedom. The price was his own life. As a result, we are now free from sin and its consequences. We have been redeemed from the slavery of sin and death.

Regathering

If both Judaism and Christianity are correct in their definitions of redemption, then Jesus must do both what Judaism is expecting the Messiah to do and what Christians expect him to do. This means that Jesus will do more than come back and save those who believe in him from sin and death. He will also regather his people Israel from exile and restore them to their land in a state of blessing and peace:

> The wilderness and the dry land shall be glad; the desert shall rejoice and blossom like the crocus; it shall blossom abundantly and rejoice with joy and singing. The glory of Lebanon shall be given to it, the majesty of Carmel and Sharon. They shall see the glory of the LORD, the majesty of our God. Strengthen the weak hands, and make firm the feeble knees. Say to those who have an anxious heart, "Be strong; fear not! Behold, your God will come with vengeance, with the recompense of God. He will come and save you." ... No lion shall be there, nor shall any ravenous beast come up on it; they shall not be found there, but the redeemed shall walk there. And the ransomed of the LORD shall return and come to Zion with singing; everlasting joy shall be upon their heads;

they shall obtain gladness and joy, and sorrow and sighing shall flee away. (Isaiah 35:1–4, 9–10)

Listen to me, O Jacob, and Israel, whom I called! I am he; I am the first, and I am the last. My hand laid the foundation of the earth, and my right hand spread out the heavens; when I call to them, they stand forth together. ... Go out from Babylon, flee from Chaldea, declare this with a shout of joy, proclaim it, send it out to the end of the earth; say, "The LORD has redeemed his servant Jacob!" They did not thirst when he led them through the deserts; he made water flow for them from the rock; he split the rock and the water gushed out. (Isaiah 48:12–13, 20–21)

Awake, awake, put on your strength, O Zion; put on your beautiful garments, O Jerusalem, the holy city; for there shall no more come into you the uncircumcised and the unclean. Shake yourself from the dust and arise; be seated, O Jerusalem; loose the bonds from your neck, O captive daughter of Zion. For thus says the LORD: "You were sold for nothing, and you shall be redeemed without money." (Isaiah 52:1–3)

"At that time, declares the LORD, I will be the God of all the clans of Israel, and they shall be my people." Thus says the LORD: "The people who survived the sword found grace in the wilderness; when Israel sought for rest, the LORD appeared to him from far away. I have loved you with an everlasting love; therefore I have continued my faithfulness to you. Again I will build you, and you shall be built, O virgin Israel! Again you shall adorn yourself with tambourines and shall go forth in the dance of the merrymakers. Again you shall plant vineyards on the mountains of Samaria; the planters shall plant and shall enjoy the fruit. For there shall be a day when watchmen will call in the hill country of Ephraim: 'Arise, and let us go up to Zion, to the LORD our God.'" (Jeremiah 31:1–6)

But you, O mountains of Israel, shall shoot forth your branches and yield your fruit to my people Israel, for they will soon come home. For behold, I am for you, and I will turn to you, and you shall be tilled and sown. And I will multiply people on you, the whole house of Israel, all of it. The cities shall be inhabited and the waste places rebuilt. (Ezekiel 36:8–10)

It is not as simple, then, as saying that Jesus is only going to come for those who believe in him. These verses are all directed toward the people of Israel, the Jewish people. God has promised to redeem them, to bring them back to the land of Israel and to bless them there.

This promise has one condition: the Jewish people must obey the message of Jesus and the prophets: "Repent of your sins; keep my commandments; obey the Torah" (see Deuteronomy 30:1–10). However, God has promised that the Jewish people will eventually listen to this message:

> Behold, the days are coming, declares the LORD, when I will make a new covenant with the house of Israel and the house of Judah, not like the covenant that I made with their fathers on the day when I took them by the hand to bring them out of the land of Egypt, my covenant that they broke, though I was their husband, declares the LORD. For this is the covenant that I will make with the house of Israel after those days, declares the LORD: I will put my law within them, and I will write it on their hearts. And I will be their God, and they shall be my people. And no longer shall each one teach his neighbor and each his brother, saying, "Know the LORD," for they shall all know me, from the least of them to the greatest, declares the LORD. For I will forgive their iniquity, and I will remember their sin no more. (Jeremiah 31:31–34)

This restoration is necessary in order to sanctify God's name:

> Therefore say to the house of Israel, Thus says the Lord GOD: It is not for your sake, O house of Israel, that I am about to act, but for the sake of my holy name, which you have profaned among the nations to which you came. And I will vindicate the holiness of my great name, which has been profaned among the nations, and which you have

profaned among them. And the nations will know that I am the LORD, declares the Lord GOD, when through you I vindicate my holiness before their eyes. I will take you from the nations and gather you from all the countries and bring you into your own land. (Ezekiel 36:22–24)

It follows that Israel's redemption is inevitable. It will happen; it is only a matter of time.

Jesus is our redeemer. He will save us from sin. But he is also the redeemer of Israel. He will save the Jewish people from all their enemies. He will, in the end, plant them back in their land and make them to live there in peace and safety. In fact, to believe in Jesus as the Messiah is to believe that he will do both of these things. That is part of the meaning of the term—but we'll get to that later.

Until the time of redemption comes, we Christians should take up the cause of the Jewish people and remember God's unfailing promises to them. This includes supporting their right to live in the land God promised them. While we don't have to agree with every action of the secular government of Israel, and we must pray for peace rather than foment war, we must also understand that the land belongs to God and that God has promised that the Jewish people will have it for an eternal inheritance.

Priest

Since then we have a great high priest who has passed through the heavens, Jesus, the Son of God, let us hold fast our confession.

— Hebrews 4:14

What's a priest? If you don't know much about Christianity, you might think that a priest is a man with a black shirt and a white collar, who isn't allowed to get married but who can absolve you of your sins. This is the popular depiction of priests in movies and books. It is loosely derived from Roman Catholicism.

For devout Catholics the parish priest is seen as the parishioner's connection with God. Catholics receive sacraments, which communicate God's grace, through the priest. The priest is, in some sense, a mediator, a messenger, a broker between the regular Catholic parishioner and the heavenly court.

All Christians, not just Catholics, believe that Jesus is our high priest. When we say this, we mean that Jesus talks to God on our behalf. Jesus is the one through whom we can have a relationship with God; without Jesus we wouldn't be able to enter God's presence.

The idea of a priest as a mediator, a go-between, wasn't invented by Jesus. The idea of priesthood goes way back to the early chapters of Genesis. Abraham was given bread and wine by the priest Melchizedek (Genesis 14:18–20). Later, in Exodus, God created a priesthood for the ancient Israelites. The priests in the Old Testament weren't much like today's Catholic priests, but they were mediators in the sense that they did something for the Israelites that the Israelites weren't allowed to do for themselves: they applied the blood of animal sacrifices to the altar at the Tabernacle and, later, at the Temple in Jerusalem.

Regular people were forbidden to apply blood to the altar in the Temple. They were also forbidden to go into the holy place of the Temple, the antechamber to God's domain. Only priests could perform the Temple duties and enter the holy place. The holy of holies, the inner sanctum of the Temple, where God's real presence dwelt, could be entered only by the high priest, and only once a year, on the Day of Atonement (Yom Kippur).

Priests weren't elected or appointed. They were—and still are—direct male-line descendants of Moses' brother, Aaron. They are called *kohanim*, from the Hebrew word *kohen*, translated "priest" in English versions of the Old Testament. Many Jews today have the last name Cohen, Coen, or some other derivative of the word *kohen*; many of these men are sons of Aaron and eligible for the priesthood.

Like God's choice to make the Jewish people his special, chosen people, it seems arbitrary for God to make Aaron's family—specifically, his male descendants—the priests of Israel. We don't know why God restricted this job to a single family or to men, but he did. This choice is permanent; it is perpetual; it never ends (Exodus 29:9, 40:15; Jeremiah 33:17–22).

Here, however, we run into a problem. Jesus was not a *kohen*. All *kohanim* were from the tribe of Levi, because Moses' brother Aaron was a Levite. But Jesus didn't come from the tribe of Levi; he came from the tribe of Judah. He didn't have "Levi's genes"; he couldn't be a priest.

Jesus never splashed an animal's blood on the altar or went into the holy place of the Temple. He didn't perform the functions of a Levitical priest. He wasn't eligible to do these things. He wasn't allowed. You would think that the Son of God could do whatever he wanted, but rules are rules, and Jesus followed them.

So if Jesus was not a *kohen*, a descendant of Aaron, then how can he be called our high priest?

Sacrifice

One of the main functions of the Levitical priests was to offer sacrifices—including animal sacrifices. Some people think that these sacrifices are icky, cruel, and unnecessary. So why were the Jewish people so big on animal sacrifices? This is a question every Christian should be able to answer, because our culture considers these practices to be archaic and even barbaric—but they're right there in our Bibles.

You've probably heard some of the objections to animal sacrifice: "Those poor animals. Why would God want us to senselessly slaughter and incinerate countless little critters? The Jews must have been confused, and Jesus came to set them straight." Or, "Thank God we don't live in that time. I could never watch an innocent animal die like that."

First of all, everyone who has ever eaten a fast-food hamburger has been responsible for the untimely demise of some poor, innocent, cud-chewing bovine.

Okay, I'm being a little facetious. But really, it is impossible for the carnivores among us to take any kind of moral high ground when it comes to killing animals. If there's nothing morally wrong with eating meat, then there's nothing morally wrong with animal sacrifice—at least in principle.

Second, we learn from the Torah that God mandated animal sacrifices (Leviticus 1–7). The Jewish people didn't come up with the idea of killing animals, splashing their blood on the altar, and cutting out the fat from around the kidneys to be burned. God himself commanded the Israelites to offer dozens of different sacrifices for a wide variety of reasons, and he told them exactly how he wanted them to do it.[46] The Jews in Jesus' time continued to be faithful to God's command, and they perpetually offered animal sacrifices at the Temple in Jerusalem.

Most Christians believe that Jesus put an end to animal sacrifices. This is easy for people to believe if they think that sacrifices are unnecessary or wrong or cruel to animals. Our modern world is okay with a Jesus who came to stop people from slaughtering thousands of sheep, goats, and bulls and setting them on fire. But this Jesus isn't the Jesus of the New Testament. This popularly conceived Jesus actually fights against God and the Bible. He takes an eraser to Scripture instead of confirming the Word of God.

Many Christians understand that God instituted animal sacrifices in the Torah. However, most of us still believe that Jesus came to change things, to get rid of animal sacrifices. Some Christians think that animal sacrifices took away sins; however, Hebrews 10:4 specifically says that they did not: "It is impossible for the blood of bulls and goats to take away sins."

Other Christians believe that the sacrifices were nothing more than dramatic pre-enactments of Jesus' death. They were like visual lessons, teaching the Jewish people that death was necessary to atone for sin so that Jesus' death would make sense to them when it happened. After Jesus died and rose again, these visual lessons were no longer necessary.

But not all sacrifices have to do with sin or atonement. Many sacrifices were offered for other reasons. Many of them were voluntary—people could bring them whenever they wanted, not necessarily for a specific reason or because of something they had done wrong.[47] In fact, Jesus almost certainly brought sacrifices to the Temple. Sacrifices were a normal part of life for any observant Jew, whether he had sinned or not.

The purpose of animal sacrifices in general was not to pay for sin (though there were offerings that had to be brought after one sinned). They were first and foremost a way of connecting with God.

D. Thomas Lancaster sums up the mystical, symbolism-laden process this way: first the worshiper placed his hands on the animal's head, symbolically transferring his identity to the animal. Then the blood of the animal, which was thought to contain its life (Leviticus 17:11), was removed (through slitting the throat) and caught in a bowl to be placed on the altar. The altar itself was thought of as a kind of portal between God's realm and ours. The life of the animal (the blood), which now represented the life of the worshiper, was placed on the altar, and symbolically, it represented the worshiper's approach to the holy, transcendent God.[48]

This may sound like something out of a weird, cultic religion. You might picture it happening at Stonehenge rather than in Jerusalem at God's holy Temple. But like it or not, this is the way God commanded his people to draw near to him.

Jesus never spoke against the sacrificial system. He prophesied the destruction of the Temple, the place where sacrifices were offered, but this was part of his prophetic rebuke to the Jewish people, a warning of what would happen if they rejected his message—we talked about this in an earlier chapter. Never did he say that sacrifices were bad, wrong, or unnecessary in themselves.

An Old Testament prophet, Jeremiah, also prophesied the destruction of the Temple—in his case, the First Temple:

> Go now to my place that was in Shiloh, where I made my name dwell at first, and see what I did to it because of the evil of my people Israel. And now, because you have done all these things, declares the LORD, and when I spoke to you persistently you did not listen, and when I called you, you did not answer, therefore I will do to the house that is called by my name, and in which you trust, and to the place that I gave to you and to your fathers, as I did to Shiloh. (Jeremiah 7:12–14)

Jeremiah later wrote, "The Levitical priests shall never lack a man in my presence to offer burnt offerings, to burn grain offerings, and to make sacrifices forever" (Jeremiah 33:18). So we have a prophecy in Jeremiah that the Temple was going to be destroyed, but this clearly didn't mean that God had put an end to animal sacrifice. So it was with Jesus' prophecy.

We know that Jesus didn't tell his disciples to quit offering sacrifices in the Temple. Jesus' disciples continued to participate in Temple worship, which included animal sacrifices, even after Jesus' ascent into heaven. When Peter and John went to the Temple at the time of the afternoon prayer (Acts 3:1), they would have been part of a ritual service including the slaughter of the *tamid* offering (Numbers 28:1–8). When Paul completed his vow (Acts 21:17–26), he would have had to offer several animals as sacrifices (Numbers 6:13–17).

So if Jesus didn't come to end animal sacrifices, what did he do? What did Jesus accomplish that animal sacrifices couldn't?

On top of that, the ideas of priesthood and sacrifice are intimately connected. So how can Jesus be a priest without offering animal sacrifices?

Supernal

According to the book of Hebrews, Jesus did something that the Levitical priests could never do. His sacrifice was of a totally different kind than the animal sacrifices God commanded in Leviticus 1–7. Whereas the blood of sacrificed animals ritually cleansed the Temple and all its accoutrements, Jesus' blood somehow directly affected the supernal realms and cleansed the heavenly Temple (Hebrews 9:23)—a mystical concept that the author of Hebrews doesn't take the time to explain fully.

The blood of animals was able to ritually cleanse the body of the worshiper, making someone clean again after contracting ritual impurity (again, these concepts are difficult to understand as they have no parallels in our modern world). However, Jesus' blood is able to cleanse the conscience of the worshiper—his inward part, his spirit, and not his body (Hebrews 9:13–14).

These differences make it clear that Jesus' sacrifice was not like the Old Testament sacrifices. It was a completely different kind of thing. When two things are completely different in their scope and power, they can coexist. One doesn't necessarily replace the other. Jesus' blood doesn't make people ritually clean or cleanse the earthly Temple; animal sacrifices would still be required to do that.

On the other hand, animal sacrifices never took away sin (Hebrews 10:4); only Jesus' sacrifice can do that. So Jesus' sacrifice doesn't replace animal sacrifices. If it had, then as my colleague Aaron Eby once said, Jesus didn't come to save us—he came to save the animals!

In the same way, Jesus' priesthood doesn't replace the Levitical priesthood. As discussed above, Moses' brother's sons were promised that priesthood forever. Instead, Jesus' priesthood is of a totally different and superior kind. Whereas Levitical priests served in the earthly Temple, which was only a copy of the heavenly one, Jesus serves in the original, heavenly Temple—the abode of God's presence in the highest place (Hebrews 8:1–2).

Jesus' ministry in the heavenly temple doesn't invalidate the earthly Temple. The same God who sent Jesus also commanded Moses to build the Tabernacle as a copy of his supernal abode (Exodus 25:9; Hebrews 8:5). It was God's idea to make an earthly shadow of the heavenly reality. There's nothing wrong with that.

Since we are no closer to seeing that mystical heavenly Temple than our ancestors were, an earthly copy would still benefit us today.

In fact, there is no reason why a Temple could not function today, complete with animal sacrifices, even after Jesus' death and resurrection. The prophet Ezekiel saw a heavenly vision of just such a Temple, one that will stand during the Messianic Age, when Jesus reigns on his throne in Jerusalem (Ezekiel 40–48). However, the reality of what Jesus accomplished is greater than the shadow or copy of that reality as depicted in the Temple sacrifices.

As our high priest, Jesus—still the Jewish carpenter and rabbi from the time of the Second Temple—currently sits at the Father's right hand and intercedes for us. By offering his life he has opened the way for us to draw near to God with his blood. The Bible doesn't go into detail on the mechanics of how this happened. It merely states that Jesus was both priest and sacrifice in a once-for-all mystical opening of the way for people to be reconciled to God forever.

This offering and priesthood entitles Jesus to be our advocate, our "defense counsel," in the heavenly courtroom. Jesus petitions God on our behalf. He argues our case. He opens the way for us to have a relationship with God. On top of that, he has cleansed our consciences and forgiven our sins, allowing us to draw near to God in a way that was never possible through animal sacrifices.

Just like the *kohanim* in the ancient Temple, Jesus is a go-between, a mediator between us and God. However, unlike the *kohanim*, Jesus doesn't have to go through any ritual process to make that connection happen. He has already done all the work. The way is open. Because of him we can have an intimate relationship with God we never could have enjoyed otherwise.

As the author of Hebrews wrote:

> Therefore, brothers, since we have confidence to enter the holy places by the blood of Jesus, by the new and living way that he opened for us through the curtain, that is, through his flesh, and since we have a great priest over the house of God, let us draw near with a true heart in full assurance of faith, with our hearts sprinkled clean from an evil conscience and our bodies washed with pure water. (Hebrews 10:19–22)

Jesus has opened the door; it's up to us to walk through it.

Son of God

Nathanael answered him, "Rabbi, you are the
Son of God! You are the King of Israel!"

— John 1:49

We are nearly to the end. In this penultimate chapter, before we delve into the discussion of Jesus' most famous title, we come to the Jesus of the theologians. The Jesus of the textbooks. The Jesus of the stained-glass windows. The Jesus of John chapter 1: the eternal Word, the preexistent Son.

John's gospel provides some of the most fertile ground in the New Testament for this kind of terminology. John begins his account of Jesus' life by delving into Jesus' mystical nature: "In the beginning was the Word" (John 1:1). Later in that same chapter, John records that when the disciple Nathanael first realized that Jesus was the Messiah, he said, "You are the Son of God!" When we read this, we imagine that Nathanael was referring to Jesus' divine identity as the Second Person of the Trinity.

Right?

After all, what else could "Son of God" mean?

Before we jump to conclusions, let's check and see if Nathanael might have been referring to the Old Testament. It might come as a surprise to some Christians that we actually encounter the term "son of God" earlier in Scripture than in the Gospel of John—much earlier. It first occurs in Genesis 6, in a passage many scholars believe refers to the ancient, forgotten kings of the pre-flood era.

It may also describe superhuman beings, members of the divine court—we would call them angels.[49]

The term pops up again in the first chapter of Job, probably also referring to angels.[50] Both here and in Genesis, the term is used in the plural; evidently God has many sons, of a sort. So the term is an ancient one used to describe superhuman (yet not, in the Old Testament, divine) beings.

Further on, in the Psalms, we find two fascinating passages that were read during the crowning of ancient Israelite kings. These "coronation psalms," like many of the other psalms, had a specific liturgical function. They were read aloud when new kings were installed in their office. Many Christians today read these coronation psalms as prophecies of the ultimate coming King, Jesus. Certainly, there is some prophetic foreshadowing in these passages. However, when they were originally written, they referred to the king of Israel, the one who was being crowned at the time.[51]

The first of these coronation psalms to mention the Son of God is Psalm 2. Verses 2–7 read as follows:

> The kings of the earth set themselves, and the rulers take counsel together, against the LORD and against his Anointed [Hebrew: *moshiach*, Messiah, the King of Israel], saying, "Let us burst their bonds apart and cast away their cords from us." He who sits in the heavens laughs; the LORD holds them in derision. Then he will speak to them in his wrath, and terrify them in his fury, saying, "As for me, I have set my King on Zion, my holy hill." I will tell of the decree: The LORD said to me, "You are my Son; today I have begotten you."

The second is Psalm 110, famously interpreted by the author of Hebrews as referring to the eternal priesthood of Christ. The meaning of the third verse has been a matter of scholarly debate for many years, but some believe that the idea that the king was begotten of God is present here just as it is in Psalm 2.[52]

The Son of God is the King of Israel.[53] To say, as Nathanael did, "You are the Son of God! You are the King of Israel!" is to say the same thing twice in different terms.

After all, we are not dealing with someone who had received some kind of New Testament revelation about the Trinity or the divine Son of God. To Nathanael, the term "Son of God" couldn't have reflected the depth of understanding of someone who had read the Gospels or the Epistles. It would have very simply meant the same thing it meant in the Old Testament: the king of Israel.[54]

But one of the most wonderful—and frustrating—things about language is that it changes. The meanings of words and phrases evolve over time. The King James Version of the Bible contains many examples of this phenomenon; it has been over four hundred years since this translation was first produced, so it provides a window into how the English language looked many centuries ago.

For example, Hebrews 4:12 in the King James Version begins, "For the word of God is quick." Reading this today, we might think that the author of Hebrews is trying to tell us about the speed of the Bible. Perhaps it is quick to help us solve our problems, or something like that.

But the word "quick" four hundred years ago referred to something that was alive. Knowing this, the translators of the English Standard Version used a different word here: "For the word of God is living." For us today this is a more accurate translation, because it uses words the way we expect them to be used.

Something similar happened with the term "Son of God" in the New Testament time period. It started off meaning nothing more than "King of Israel." However, as time passed, and as his followers realized that Jesus was more than just a human king, the title "Son of God" came to reflect a newly discovered reality. The Son of God was identified with the Word of God (John 1:1–3), a concept that finds its roots in ancient Judaism.

Word

God is supernal and transcendent. He is utterly above anything that we can imagine.

But sometimes the Bible is a little ambivalent on that point. Sometimes God is described as having arms or wings. Sometimes he is described as looking like a human. Sometimes he is described as having emotions just like ours and as changing his mind about things he has done.

This didn't sit well with many pious Jews in the years before Jesus walked the earth. So as they translated the Old Testament into the language of the common people, Aramaic (these translations are called Targums), they took many of these anthropomorphisms—statements that made God out to be like a human—and transferred them to another entity called "the *Memra* [Word] of the LORD."[55]

The *Memra*, or Word, was like an extension of God without being exactly the same as God. It had God's characteristics and God's power and could act on God's behalf, but it was somehow removed from the very person of God.

When John wrote the prologue to his gospel, he chose this same terminology—the *Memra*, the Word:

> In the beginning was the Word, and the Word was with God, and the Word was God. He was in the beginning with God. All things were made through him, and without him was not any thing made that was made. In him was life, and the life was the light of men. The light shines in the darkness, and the darkness has not overcome it. (John 1:1–5)

Some scholars believe that John was referencing the Targums and their use of the word *Memra* when he described Jesus as the "Word of God."[56] If this is the case, then John identified Jesus with the mysterious presence that seemed to be God's agent throughout the Old Testament.

John wrote many years after Jesus' life and ministry, toward the end of the first century. He had a lot of time before writing his gospel to think about all the things that Jesus had said and done. Knowing this, it shouldn't surprise us that John takes us deeper into Jesus' nature than do the other gospels. It probably took some time for the apostles to make the connection between Jesus and the *Memra* of the Old Testament, but once they did, it became a powerful way to describe the person and nature of Jesus.

Incarnate

As the apostles grew to understand that Jesus had been more than just a man and more than just a rabbi and more than just the Messiah King, at some point they recognized that the ancient designation for Israelite kings, "Son of God," may have held a deeper meaning than they first imagined.

After all, the angels were called sons of God even before the kings of Israel, so there was a precedent for believing that the term could refer to a supernatural being.

As time went on, the title "Son of God" grew to describe the unique relationship that Jesus enjoyed with God. Not just a king of Israel but an "only begotten Son," an unprecedented kind of person—a person who was also divine.

Many of the ancient kings of the pagan nations had imagined themselves to be gods, from Pharaoh to Caesar. But Jesus was seen as the realization of this idea. A king who was more than a king; a man who was more than a man.

So while Nathanael may have only meant "king of Israel" when he first called Jesus the Son of God, John, with sixty or seventy years of hindsight, recognized that there was more to the story than Nathanael could have known at the time.

Many similar events, sayings, and titles for Jesus appear only in John, probably because it was not until John's time that their significance was fully realized. It took many years for Jesus' followers to process and think through everything that he had said and done among them.

As Christian theology developed, in the very early years of the church, the idea that Jesus is the preexistent Word, or *Memra*, was coupled with the idea that Jesus is the unique Son of God. Each of these terms has multiple shades of meaning and deep roots in the Old Testament. Together, they form a powerful picture of a preexistent divine being, related to God and yet not the same person as God but nonetheless God himself, who had been active throughout the history of creation and who had somehow taken human form to reveal God to humanity.

From this seed grew the Christology of the church. The Trinity, the Incarnation, the hypostatic union, and other formulations were enshrined in creeds (and countless other terms were tried and discarded) as the early church fathers attempted to describe what may, in the end, be impossible to understand, much less put into words: the unprecedented and unique relationship between Jesus and the Father.

It would not be too much of a stretch to state that it was on these mysteries that the church chose to debate and meditate for several centuries after the resurrection. The outworking of these debates shaped the church for hundreds of years to come.

Messiah

He asked them, "But who do you say that I am?"
Peter answered him, "You are the Christ."

— Mark 8:29

Everyone knows that Jesus is called "the Christ." In fact, the title has become so attached to him that some people think it's part of his name—as if "Mary Christ" married "Joseph Christ" and had "Jesus Christ."

Jesus didn't grow up as "Little Jesus Christ." He was "Yeshua ben Yosef"—Jesus, son of Joseph (Galilean Jews didn't often have surnames, or last names, back then). "Christ" is actually a title, like "King Jesus" or "Lord Jesus."

The title "Christ" didn't originally mean anything in English; it's not even an English word. It's an ancient Greek word (*christos*). In Greek it means "anointed," as in "You anoint my head with oil" (Psalm 23:5) or "I anointed my hair with shampoo this morning." (We don't normally "christen," or anoint, people much anymore—at least, not the way we used to.)

"Jesus Christ" means "Jesus the Anointed One." But what is the significance of this anointing?

It turns out that the term "Christ" (Hebrew: *Mashiach*, usually transliterated "Messiah") is an extremely important one. It ties together many of the concepts we have already looked at in this book. Jesus' kingship, his important message and calling, his function as the redeemer of Israel, and even his atoning death are all encapsulated in that one term.

How can one word mean so much?

The term "Messiah" was invested with extreme significance in Jesus' time, far beyond what it meant in the Old Testament. The word "Messiah" in the Old Testament, usually translated in our Bibles as "anointed" or "anointed one," almost always refers to the king of Israel. Each king was anointed with oil to symbolize his investiture, his "christening"—the beginning of his reign. Probably the most famous example of this is when Samuel anointed David as the future king when David was just a shepherd boy (1 Samuel 16:1–13).

"Messiah" appears again in the coronation psalms discussed in the last chapter. In the Psalms the Messiah is the anointed King of Israel, but he is also mysteriously referred to as God's Son. The next time the word is mentioned in Scripture, it is used of King Cyrus (Isaiah 45:1), the famous Persian king who released the Jews from exile so they could return home to Israel. A few chapters later, Isaiah prophesies the coming of another anointed one, a man who will bring the good news of Israel's final redemption (Isaiah 61:1). After that, the term shows up again in Daniel chapter 9, referring to the mysterious "Anointed Prince." Another brief mention in Habakkuk 3:13, and then "Messiah" is gone.

From these verses Judaism found a name—*Mashiach*, or Messiah—for its rich tradition of a coming king from an ancient bloodline, one who would restore the throne of David, bring the Jewish people back from exile, inaugurate world peace, and righteously enforce the Law of Moses over the people of Israel.

These concepts are scattered throughout the prophetic literature. Ezekiel recorded God's promise that Israel will be restored (Ezekiel 36) and that "David shall be king over them" (Ezekiel 37:24). Jeremiah prophesied that God's covenant with David would one day be renewed and established forever—that his descendants would rule over Israel forever (Jeremiah 33:14–26). These and countless other passages that describe a future state of blessing and peace were understood in Jesus' time to refer to a single period of time, today called the Messianic Age, in which Israel's King would reign supreme.

If you know anything about Jesus' second coming, these prophecies might sound familiar to you. There is another set of prophecies that you probably know even better—prophecies such as Isaiah 53, which foretells the death of God's Anointed One for the sins of God's people. Jesus fulfilled these prophecies when he died on the cross.

Christs

It seems obvious to us now that the Jesus who died on the cross for our sins is the very same Jesus who is going to come again in glory. But looking at the two sets of prophecies, one about a very important person who dies and one about an anointed king, the Jewish people came up with the idea of two Messiahs—two Christs. One Messiah was *Mashiach ben Yosef*—Messiah, son of Joseph. Like the Bible hero Joseph, this Messiah would encounter unmerited hardship. Eventually, he would be killed.

The other Messiah was *Mashiach ben David*—Messiah, son of David. This Messiah was the one who was going to rule over Israel during the blessed Messianic Age. Many Bible scholars speculate that in Jesus' time, the Jewish people were only expecting the Son of David. They wanted someone who would break the yoke of the Roman oppressors from their neck and lead them to victory in battle. They wanted a king so badly that they missed the humble servant God sent them.

This might be true on some level. However, many Christian commentators take this idea to an extreme. They teach that the Jewish expectation of a ruling, conquering Messiah King was completely wrong. They teach that the Jews missed their Messiah, Jesus, because they were deluded into thinking that God actually cared about their national destiny, when in reality, God never intended to redeem the Jewish people.

This kind of thinking is totally backwards. God promised the Jewish people an anointed king who would redeem them from their enemies. These promises can be found in nearly every prophetic book of the Old Testament, from Isaiah (9:1–7) through Malachi (3:1–4). The Jewish expectation of a Messiah King was (and continues to be) completely biblical.

Because of Judaism's traditional belief in two Messiahs, many religious Jews today believe that, at the end of this age, there will be a Joseph-like figure who dies for his people and a David-like figure who will gather the Jewish people back into their land and bring a new world of prosperity and peace.

This is incredibly important—I don't want anyone to miss it. Jewish tradition, based on the same Bible verses that we see in the Old Testament about a suffering servant, expects a Messiah-figure who looks an awful lot like Jesus.

When I first learned this, it blew me away. It's not just the Jewish Bible (the Old Testament) that speaks of a coming Messiah who will give his life for his people. Even Jewish traditions from later time periods speak of this self-sacrificial figure. The Jewish people are sitting right on top of a gold mine of prophecies and traditions that point directly to Jesus Christ.

I can't help but think that at the right time, this will become obvious to the observant Jewish community. Even now, many religious Jews have begun to understand that when Jesus is seen as he originally was—as an observant Jew—then the door will finally be open for him to be recognized as the promised Messiah. These Messianic Jews have formed a growing, thriving religious movement in Israel and in the United States.

Many speculate—although there is absolutely no way to confirm this—that even more religious Jews have understood these things and know who Jesus is but have not told anyone their beliefs, because if they admitted to being followers of Jesus, they would be ostracized from the Jewish community and shunned by all their family and friends.

How can this be? Why does this simple shift—the understanding that Jesus was an observant Jew—make it so much easier for Jews to accept him as their Messiah? And if Jesus was a pious Jew, then why was Jesus rejected by the Jewish people in his own time? After all, they knew him firsthand; they should have known that he was scrupulously observant of the laws and traditions of his people.

Promises

Most people are surprised to learn that the reason many of Jesus' contemporaries rejected him is totally different from the reason most modern Jews reject him.

This is because most people think that Jesus came to get rid of Judaism, to tell the Jews they were no longer God's chosen people, and to replace them with Christians and Christianity. If this were true, then it would make sense for Jews to reject Jesus in his time and to continue rejecting him now. After all, how would a Christian feel if someone claimed to be from God and said, "God is sick and tired of you Christians—you're doing a terrible job. He's going to replace you with someone else, and now you can be saved only if you convert to _____"—some other religion? If you're a committed Christian, then you know that can't happen—God has made promises to us through Jesus that no one can ever take away.

Well, God has also made promises to the children of Abraham, Isaac, and Jacob—promises that no one can take away. Many Christians seem to think that Jesus came to break those promises and to remove the Jewish people from their traditional role as God's chosen people. After all, how many pastors teach that when Jesus returns, he will renew his unique relationship with the "clans of Israel" (Jeremiah 31:1), giving them a new covenant in which their blessing and obedience to God are guaranteed (31:31–34)? Most of the time, these kinds of promises are simply appropriated for Christians; the Jewish people are left out of the picture.

Other Christians have taught that the Jewish people never had any special status before God and are actually on God's "naughty list." This idea was enshrined in the literature of the ancient church fathers: Justin Martyr called Christians the "true spiritual Israel"[57] and claimed that the Law of Moses had been given to the Jewish people as a curse.[58]

How about that. The special, unique love that God proclaimed to the children of Israel—an everlasting love (Jeremiah 31:3)—somehow transformed, in early church theology, to a spiteful curse.

Every day, as part of the evening liturgical prayers of Orthodox Judaism, hundreds of thousands of religious Jews recite the *Ahavat Olam* prayer, which begins, "With an everlasting love have you loved us," echoing the language of Jeremiah and the other prophets. Is it any wonder that these Jews reject a Jesus who is supposed to have taught that God no longer loves the Jewish people as his unique and special covenant nation?

Many Christians have also traditionally taught that Jesus came to do away with the Law of Moses, the Torah—or at least large sections of it. Famous early Christian orator John Chrysostom said, "Jews so revere the Law, that although the time has come which annuls it, they still contend for the observance of all its contents, contrary to the purpose of God."[59] We have already discussed how central the Law was to the life, practice and teaching of Jesus.

But if Jesus didn't really teach these anti-Jewish ideas, why did his people reject him?

Stumble

Why did Jesus' people reject him?

The first part of the answer is—they didn't. At least, not all of them did. The church in Jerusalem, which was initially made up completely of Jews[60] who worshiped daily in the Temple (Acts 2:46, 3:1, 5:12), was a large and influential Jewish sect (Acts 5:13–16) up until the First Jewish War, forty years after the Resurrection, when they were forced to flee the country, as Jesus instructed them to do in Luke 21:20–24. Even after that time Jewish believers in Jesus continued to live and practice their faith for centuries, though they were scattered throughout the Roman Empire.[61]

But what about the rest of the Jewish people? Why didn't they accept Jesus?

We can answer that question in a few ways. The earthly, political reality of the situation was that Jesus posed a threat to those in power in Jerusalem in those days. The Sadducees, corrupt priests who had bowed the knee to Rome and accumulated vast wealth from the Temple coffers, held powerful positions on the Sanhedrin. Allied with the corrupt Herodians and some hypocritical, wealthy Pharisees, this power bloc did whatever they could to maintain the status quo. The Sadducees, Herodians, and other powerful and wealthy men knew that if the peace with Rome were to be broken, their fortunes would be totally lost.

Jesus had the potential to be the greatest disturber of the peace that the world had ever seen. Sure, he was prophesied to be the Prince of Peace—but this title only applies when he is reigning on his throne, enforcing peace and justice throughout the world. If he would have taken up the sword and fought the nations of the world for dominance, as the Messiah is prophesied to do, he would have upset the delicate balance of power that had allowed a few corrupt Jewish leaders to accumulate massive wealth.

The Sadducees, the major power players on the Sanhedrin (due to the wealth and influence attached to the Temple), didn't believe in an afterlife or in eternal punishment or reward. They paid no mind to the prophecies of Israel's national restoration. In their minds they literally had nothing to lose by killing Jesus, and everything to gain.

These leaders had means at their disposal to manipulate Jesus' trial—influence, money, and manpower. They had Jesus arrested and brought to the personal residence of the high priest, where they illegally extracted a confession that Jesus was the Messiah— the coming King. With this, they felt that they could convince the Roman provincial government that Jesus was a threat to Rome, a usurper, a self-proclaimed competitor to the Emperor Tiberius.

The Roman prefect, Pontius Pilate, saw through the Sadducees' charade. He began planning to release Jesus, in keeping with a Jewish tradition that a prisoner be granted clemency on Passover Eve. This, he thought, would free his hand to crucify a truly dangerous enemy to Rome, the recently apprehended rebel, insurrectionist, and murderer, Barabbas. However, Pilate was outmaneuvered.

The Sadducees and their cohorts began by stocking the crowd in Pilate's Praetorium with their own people on the morning of Passover Eve. They knew that Barabbas' friends, the Zealots, would also be there clamoring for his release. At the opportune moment, when Pilate brought Barabbas before them, they joined their voices with those of the Zealots—"Release him!" Then, when presented with Jesus, they were the first to shout "Crucify him!"[62] In this way, "like sheep without a shepherd" (Mark 6:34), the people of Israel were betrayed by their own self-interested, short-sighted leaders, who rejected the very person who could have broken Israel's chains.

But through all this we know that God had a bigger plan. In Romans 11 Paul reflected that God had allowed the Jewish people as a whole to reject Jesus because God wanted to give non-Jews a chance to be part of God's people, to be beneficiaries of God's gracious covenants with Israel. Paul went on to explain that Israel's unbelief is only temporary—it's sort of like a stumble, like when you're walking down the sidewalk and trip over your shoes and just manage to catch yourself.

God allowed Israel to stumble in order to give a brief period of time for Gentiles to get on board with God's program. In the end, both Jesus-believing Gentiles and the Jewish nation will be saved; and while this does not guarantee the salvation of every single Jewish person (see, for example, Matthew 3:7–10), the Apostle Paul affirms that God will have a comprehensive kind of mercy on his people Israel (Romans 11:26, 32).

Light

Paul refers to the death of the Messiah, the stumbling of Israel, and the opening of the door to the Gentiles as a mystery that had only recently been revealed. But God had hinted at this plan long before. Isaiah 49:6 records a prophetic oracle in which God explicitly tells his people that their Messiah, their beloved Bridegroom, their Rescuer and Savior, would be more than they could ever imagine:

> It is too light a thing that you should be my servant to raise up the tribes of Jacob and to bring back the preserved of Israel; I will make you as a *light for the nations*, that my salvation may reach to the end of the earth (emphasis added).

Rather than send two Messiahs, as many Jews were expecting, God sent one Messiah with two missions. One mission was to restore the Jewish people, to "raise up the tribes of Jacob and bring back the preserved of Israel." Jesus will complete this mission at his second coming.

The other mission, the "secret" mission that no one really figured out until later on, was to be a "light for the nations." Jesus accomplished this in a way that no one expected—even though God had Isaiah write it down hundreds of years beforehand: "Behold, my servant shall act wisely; he shall be high and lifted up, and shall be exalted ... he shall sprinkle many nations; kings shall shut their mouths because of him." This is the beginning of the "suffering servant" passage, the verses that immediately precede Isaiah 53, the most explicit Old Testament account of Jesus' crucifixion.

Jesus' self-sacrifice, his giving up of himself to death on the cross, has inspired an uncountable number of people to cleave to the God of Abraham. Jesus has truly been a light to the nations. He has rallied millions and millions—even billions—of people to God's cause.

Now Jesus is poised to finish his other mission—to restore the tribes of Jacob. He will come again, the Jewish rabbi-turned-king, and the people of Israel will accept him as their ruler. Most Christians think that this will be because of his supernatural arrival, his descent from heaven on a white horse (Revelation 19:11–16). After all, who would deny Jesus after seeing him in his glory, transfigured into his supernatural divine form?

However, if Jesus really came to get rid of Judaism and the Torah, the Jewish people wouldn't accept him even if he returned in his full glory. Religious Jews faithfully hold to Deuteronomy 13:1–5, which states that even a miracle-working prophet cannot be accepted if he leads his people to disobey the Law of Moses, and to Deuteronomy 17:8–13, which states that any Jew who rejects the legal rulings of the Jewish leadership—which today exist as the collected traditions of the Jewish people—is to be put to death (today, exiled from the community). The Jesus of Justin Martyr and John Chrysostom will never hold water with the Jewish faithful. More importantly, this Jesus cannot be the Messiah, because he fails to live up to the promises God made. He disqualifies himself by breaking God's rules.

Fortunately for those of us who have put our faith in Jesus of Nazareth, this other Jesus who rejects Jews and Judaism doesn't exist. The Jewish people will accept Jesus at his second coming because it will be clear to them that Jesus is—not just was, but *is*—a faithful, observant Jew who has been sent by God to redeem and restore his people.

Today the first fruits of this realization have begun to mature. Messianic Judaism is experiencing growth and revival as it has not seen since the first century. Biblical scholars are writing book after book on how Jesus was an observant Jewish rabbi who came to affirm rather than to annul the Law of Moses, who came to restore rather than to condemn the people of Israel.

By spreading the word that Jesus was an observant, faithful Jew, we can bring the world one step closer to the final redemption. We can open the door for the Jewish people to recognize their Messiah—if not now, then at least when he returns again in glory. We can repair Jesus' reputation, which has been damaged by years of misunderstanding.

We can start today.

Part 3

The Journey forward

Unforeseen Consequences

To wrench Jesus out of his Jewish world destroys
Jesus and destroys Christianity.

— *Anthony J. Saldarini*

At the beginning of this book, I wrote that our lack of knowledge of Jesus is causing problems that are bigger than we can imagine.

Now that we have reexamined Jesus, who he is, and what he's like, we're ready to start looking at those problems.

A few pages ago we described discipleship in Jesus' time. A Jewish person in the first century would have understood that a disciple's relationship with his master touched every area of his life. A disciple would change everything about the way he lived in order to be more like his master.

But today, according to the Barna Research Group, less than one in every five American Christians has made discipleship the "most serious commitment" in their lives.[63]

Therefore, in the United States, for every churched person that is a seriously committed disciple, there are four more who have let discipleship slip from their first priority down to second, third, or fourth place—and beyond. In the lives of these halfhearted believers, discipleship to Jesus is taking a back seat to relationships, jobs, and personal pursuits.

But when someone says that discipleship is a low priority for them, they use the word "discipleship" in a way that it was never intended to be used. We have learned that the definition of "disciple," the way Jesus would have used that word (or its ancient Hebrew or Aramaic equivalent), doesn't leave any room for anything else to be more important. A disciple's whole life revolves around his master.

To say "Discipleship is not my most serious commitment" is to say "I'm not really a disciple."

I'm not saying that people who make this statement aren't saved or that they're going to hell or anything like that. I have no idea about that, and I don't get to decide anyway.

I'm just saying that they're not disciples. They don't fulfill the criteria.

So—what are we doing? What is the church in America doing if we're not making disciples?

We call the church the body of Christ, and it is, but if Christ isn't our first priority, and Christ is not at the center of our lives, then how can he be at the center of our church life? And if Christ isn't at the center of our church life, what *is* at the center? The music? The building? The furniture? A strategic growth plan? Vision? Liturgy? *Theology*?

If a bunch of people who are mostly not disciples come together to hear about Jesus for an hour a week but don't really follow him seriously, does that even *count* as church?

Being a Christian, back when this whole thing started in Jerusalem and Antioch and Ephesus, used to mean embracing a fully dedicated life of faith. But for most Christians in America today, "Christian" is just another label. The powerful medicine of our message has been diluted; it's been watered down. Is it any wonder that Christianity is losing its power and relevance in American culture?

Data gathered by the Pew Research Center shows that more and more Americans have no religion. They aren't looking for one, either. As I write this, Christian leaders in America are wrinkling their eyebrows over the "Rise of the 'Nones'"[64]—the increasing number of people who have no religious affiliation. Every generation has more "nones" than the generation before it. Every year the balance tips a little further.

At the time of this writing, the most recent poll I can find claims that 23 percent of Americans are "not at all" religious—a number that has doubled in the past six years.[65]

As each generation comes closer to fully rejecting Christianity, we are losing our impact. We are losing any platform we ever had in our culture. Conservative Christians are worried about the removal of the Ten Commandments from public places in America, but this is just one small symptom—it is the tip of an iceberg. The underlying cultural shift is far more massive, and it is continuing to accelerate. If current trends continue, we will quickly find ourselves becoming even less effective at reaching unchurched people with the gospel. With fewer converts come fewer resources—money, volunteer time, and everything else that a church needs to survive and thrive—and fewer evangelists.

We're in a death spiral.

Why is the church in America failing to reach so many people? Why have we been failing for several decades? Why do we continue to fail?

It has nothing to do with being seeker friendly. It has nothing to do with the style of music being played or the style of preaching of the pastor or the style of the worship service. These superficial things aren't the real issue. The color of the carpet in your sanctuary is not keeping your church from being what God has called it to be. Actually, the fact that Christians argue over these non-issues tells me that we have forgotten what is really important.

The reason that young people in America don't want to join us as disciples of Jesus is because most of us aren't disciples of Jesus.

Today's young adults want something real or nothing at all. All this talk of following somebody, with little or no actual following going on, is a turnoff.

Pointless bickering, "worship wars," intergenerational conflict, interdenominational conflict—these things only make the problem worse. They tell the world that we are partisans, not followers; we are more concerned with ideology than with discipleship.

And let's be honest: if we're not really committed to discipleship, we can't expect anyone else to commit to it either.

Because so many of us are not really committed to discipleship, many churches in America have become nothing more than social clubs, no different from the Rotary or the Elks or the Moose or the Masons. And like these other organizations, the local church is losing its relevance in a culture that is moving toward new ways of building relationships.

But what is the root of this problem? Why are we not committed to discipleship?

Because we have not encountered the real historical person of Jesus. We can't be disciples if we don't have a rabbi.

Without the Jewish rabbi, Yeshua of Nazareth, at the center of our faith, we have nothing. We are just another community organization, a country club without a golf course, an empty shell of what two thousand years ago was the most real and vital and incredible group of people on the planet.

Acculturation

It gets worse.

The real disciples, the ones who *do* prioritize discipleship as their most serious commitment, the one out of five, don't always follow who they're supposed to be following.

They have gotten into their discipleship cars and slammed the gas pedal to the floor. They are seriously committed. They are going somewhere. And most of them are very sure that the direction they have chosen is the right one.

But how many of them really know and understand the Jesus they are trying so hard to follow?

I don't have any survey data to answer that question. But I do know that before I saw the Jewish Jesus, I was headed down the wrong road. And I've met enough other believers to know that this problem is almost universal—although it affects all of us to different degrees.

It's hard to see at first because this problem, this misunderstanding of Jesus, is subtle. You can have all the right doctrine, all the right beliefs; you can be totally "orthodox"; you can pass under the radar of any test of Christian commitment and still fail here.

You can be a committed disciple and still be on the wrong track and never know it.

This disease is hard to diagnose. But there are a few symptoms that should tell us what is brewing beneath the surface of Christianity in America.

Consider the entrance of religion into American politics. Most politically active Christians naturally believe that Jesus would endorse their political positions. If they didn't think that Jesus would agree with their politics, they would change their politics—at least, if they were really serious about following Jesus.

We might think that our tendency to read our own political views back onto Jesus is simply a harmless truism, something that naturally comes with the territory—it's part of the American way of life.

However, when we attempt to bring Jesus into the ballot box, despite our good intentions we tend to infuse the already-polarizing discourse of politics with the heady self-justifying confidence of religious belief. If we really believe that Jesus agrees with our politics, then we can come to believe that our political enemies are fighting against Jesus. Political arguments then become holy wars, and our political opponents become demons.

Even worse, if we misrepresent Jesus as a Republican or a Democrat, we fail to show the world what Jesus was really like—he wasn't either of those things. And if we're really following Republican Jesus or Democrat Jesus instead of Rabbi Jesus, but we still claim to be disciples, then we misrepresent ourselves—we've lost sight of the real historical person of Jesus, the rabbi we are supposed to be following.

Or consider the tendency, stronger since the 1960s than ever before, to see Jesus as someone who is against strict religious law, as a free spirit who does whatever he feels led to do. This Disney-fied "Jiminy Cricket" Jesus—"Let your conscience be your guide!"—is one of the most popular images of Jesus in America.

Someone who believes in this Jesus will allow themselves to live a free-spirited kind of life. How seriously do you think they will take the demands of the New Testament? How rigorous, how dedicated can we expect them to be when it comes to following the commandments of Jesus and the apostles?

The opposite, by the way, is also true. If we see Jesus as nothing more than a harsh taskmaster, we will miss the grace of God and the beauty of Jesus' love for the Jewish people and, ultimately, for all humanity. If we fail to grasp the love and grace that Jesus has extended to us, we won't extend that love and grace to others.

If we are committed disciples, if we really want to be who God has called us to be, if we are intentional in any way about discipleship, we will try to be like Jesus. But something else will actually happen: we will become what we think Jesus is like. And if our mental picture of Jesus looks the way it does because we have placed some of ourselves into him, because we have created Jesus in our image instead of seeing the historical Jesus for who he was (and is), then what results is an amplification effect in which we become more like ourselves rather than more like Jesus.

In a self-reinforcing spiral, we become more committed Republicans or Democrats, we become more authoritarian or more permissive, but we fail to become more like Jesus.

Over time, we slowly acculturate—we become more like the culture around us as we begin to believe that Jesus would live and operate in our culture in the same way we would. Instead of us becoming like Christ, we make Christ look like us. We make Jesus fit into Christianity instead of reshaping Christianity to look the way Jesus would have wanted it.

Jesus should be our foundation, our rock, our anchor, our cornerstone—a fixed, immovable point. But when we don't see Jesus clearly, he becomes moldable and changeable. Discipleship becomes a moving target.

It reminds me of the story of a man who was walking through the forest. Every so often he would see an arrow shot right into the center of a bull's-eye. He marveled at the accuracy of the master archer who had hit every shot so precisely. Finally, when he caught up with the archer, he saw the truth—the archer shot at a tree, and then painted a bull's-eye where the arrow hit.

We don't do it on purpose. We don't realize we're doing it. But when we make Jesus more like us instead of becoming more like the real flesh-and-blood historical person of Jesus, we are just like that archer. Some of us are aiming for Republican Jesus or Democrat Jesus. Some of us are aiming for Jacked Manly Jesus or In-Touch-With-His-Feminine-Side Jesus. And we think that we are good disciples because we are becoming like that Jesus, but we painted that Jesus in our minds because he was already kind of like us. We hit the target because we painted it after we shot our arrow.

Eventually, we get to the point where we're not becoming more like Jesus at all.

Systemic

This not-knowing-Jesus disease is systemic. It has infected every denomination, every church, at every level.

As a result, Christianity—at least in America, where I live—is sick. We are dying because we have failed to cure this sickness.

I believe that Jesus is the cure. In fact, I believe that everything wrong with Christianity today can be traced back to our failure to really, truly know Jesus.

Pick anything; pick any one of the legitimate gripes unchurched people have about Christians.

Why do some Christians display offensive and derogatory signs? Why do they believe that God hates homosexuals?

Because they don't realize that Jesus and the apostles taught within a Jewish environment, in which everyone knew what was expected of them. Jesus taught people who had been born into Judaism and raised under Jewish law; Paul wrote to men and women who had decided to follow Jesus as Gentiles. Either way, the original readers and hearers of the New Testament were already committed to following Jewish sexual mores. They categorically accepted God's laws regarding permissible and forbidden sex. Knowing this, it is easier to see how Jesus and the apostles were fully justified in holding their audience to that commitment.

Paul could write about "men committing shameless acts with men and receiving in themselves the due penalty for their error" (Romans 1:27) because he was preaching to the choir. When he taught people who had not committed to follow Jesus, as in Acts 17:22–31, he focused on a very different issue—the identity of God. Before people are clear on the identity of God, there is no point in telling them about their specific sins. Before someone decides to follow Jesus, we aren't allowed to hold them to the same standard to which we are supposed to hold ourselves. As Paul wrote earlier in his life, in 1 Corinthians 5:12, "What have I to do with judging outsiders?"

When we read some of the tougher passages in the New Testament without Jesus' Jewishness in mind, we can sometimes imagine that Jesus and his apostles were policing the world, telling everyone how sinful they were and correcting their mistakes. But Jesus and his apostles only policed people who shared their same religious foundation: Jewish people and Gentile believers in Jesus.

Another one: why have Christians split up into so many denominations, and why do we spend so much time fighting each other over these divisions?

Because we have defined ourselves by the beliefs and practices that make us different from each other and not simply as disciples of Rabbi Jesus who live according to his teachings.

A disciple of Jesus is someone who memorizes Jesus' teachings, imitates Jesus' actions, and raises up more disciples of Jesus. But it isn't so simple to be a Methodist or a Baptist or a Presbyterian or a Lutheran.

These different schools of faith all interpret Jesus' teachings in different ways. However, historically, none of them have seen Jesus' teachings in a Jewish context. When these denominations were founded, Christians just didn't have the archaeology or the access to other Jewish texts or the depth and breadth of scholarship to be able to see the historical person of Jesus, the Jewish rabbi behind the text.

I'm not slamming these denominations—I don't assign blame to the great theologians of earlier generations who may have made mistakes because they didn't have the resources we have today. I'm just saying that when we don't see Jesus clearly, we have to decide how to fill in the gaps in order to try to follow him; throughout history, different denominations have found different ways to fill in those gaps.

These denominations each now have their own take on Jesus—a Catholic Jesus, an Anabaptist Jesus, or what have you—and each picture of Jesus reflects the teachings of its respective denomination. We are all trying to follow the same person, but we are all going about it in different ways, because none of us have clearly seen the historical figure we are supposed to be following. Instead we all filter the gospel accounts through the theological lens of our church or our denomination—or maybe we have built our own lens—and we all end up with different pictures of Jesus.

What would happen to all the division, all the infighting, if we all understood Jesus within his historical Jewish context? What would happen if all of us saw the same Jesus when we read the Gospels?

How long would it take for us to realize that we have all gotten something wrong, and that we would be better off united than divided?

I could name any number of other issues in the church. Most of them would be widely acknowledged as serious problems by the majority of committed Christians. But while Christian leaders, writers, speakers, and pastors have been focusing on these symptoms—bigotry, schisms, politicization, the shrinking church, and so many others—we have missed the disease. We have missed the fact that we clearly do not know our Master very well, and we have not made the effort that we really need to make to get to know him better.

Repair

I don't believe that Christianity is beyond hope—not by a long shot. In fact, to quote Bill Hybels of Willow Creek Community Church, I believe that the local church, the body of Christ, is the hope of the world.

But I do think we have some work to do.

Both in theology and in praxis—in belief and in practice—we have built the institutional church around a picture of Jesus that is incomplete. Once we begin to see the complete picture, we are going to realize that we have to change some things about that institution, about the church, so that we can better reflect the historical person of Jesus in the way we do Christianity and the way we do church.

We have to reach into history, take hold of the historical person of Jesus, and pull him into our churches and into our spiritual lives and let him revive and restore and renew us.

In reassessing my own life of faith in response to learning that Jesus was an observant Jew, I eventually settled on four principles that I did not follow before but that I needed to implement in order to get my life of discipleship back on track. These principles are very broad and cover an incredibly large swath of faith and practice. I think they probably apply to some degree in the lives of all Christians who have not yet seen the Jewish Jesus.

In this book I will not go further than simply to introduce each one of them. The following books in this series will explore these topics in much greater detail.

In order to repair our churches and our lives of faith, we must (1) support the Jewish people, (2) embrace a life of spiritual discipline, (3) recover the gospel of the kingdom of heaven, and (4) do whatever we can to restore the church's picture of Jesus to the historical reality of Jesus' incarnate person—the Rabbi from Nazareth.

Principle 1
Support the Jewish People

I will bless those who bless you, and him who dishonors you I will curse.

— Genesis 12:3

O ne of the biggest decisions I made in response to finding out that Jesus was a practicing Jew was to express my support of and love for the Jewish people in a tangible way.

I began to give to Jewish charities.

For me, the opportunity first arose when I was sitting in a pew at Beth Immanuel Sabbath Fellowship, a Messianic synagogue in Hudson, Wisconsin, eavesdropping on a conversation between Rabbi Dr. Michael Schiffman and another attendee at the conference for which we had all gathered.

Dr. Schiffman is the president of Chevra Humanitarian, an organization that gives no-strings-attached material aid to Holocaust survivors and other poverty-stricken Jews in the former Soviet Union and elsewhere. In the conversation I overheard, he was discussing opportunities that had arisen for his organization—people he had recently become aware of who needed help—and he was lamenting the fact that donors were hard to come by.

In that moment it became clear to me that I needed to contribute toward this cause. I don't often receive direct, specific communications from God; generally he leads me to make the best decision I can based on the Bible and on the circumstances I am in. But this time it was almost as if I got a memo from the Almighty. Give this much, every month, starting today.

It was more than I could afford.

And yet even after I started giving, my financial situation somehow didn't deteriorate.

In connection with that event, a Bible passage was brought to my attention that confirmed what God had put on my heart that day. It comes from the Epistle to the Romans:

> Macedonia and Achaia have been pleased to make some contribution for the poor among the saints at Jerusalem. For they were pleased to do it, and indeed they owe it to them. For if the Gentiles have come to share in their spiritual blessings, they ought also to be of service to them in material blessings. (Romans 15:26–27)

I was struck by Paul's words here. I had never before heard the principle that Paul invoked here in order to garner collections for poverty-stricken Jews in Jerusalem.

But once we realize that Jesus was Jewish, Paul's admonition starts to make sense. All of our spiritual knowledge, all of the blessings we inherit, and even our righteous standing before God—all of this comes through the Jewish people. To deny this would be to deny that these things come through Jesus himself, a Jew of the tribe of Judah, and the King of Israel.

Paul reckoned that non-Jewish believers owe a debt to the Jewish people because of the immense blessings we have been given in Christ. Not some kind of conceptual or spiritual debt either. We owe them "material blessings." Food, clothing, shelter.

This idea may sound strange, even bizarre. It doesn't make sense to us to exchange spiritual benefits for monetary gain. That kind of transaction invites cynicism in our post-Christian culture.

But supporting the Jewish people in this way is only one part of a much larger symbiotic relationship between the Jewish people and the nations of the world. As a "nation of priests," the Jewish people were tasked to bring the knowledge of God to the rest of the world:

> See, I have taught you statutes and rules, as the LORD my God commanded me, that you should do them in the land that you are entering to take possession of it.

Keep them and do them, for that will be your wisdom and your understanding in the sight of the peoples, who, when they hear all these statutes, will say, "Surely this great nation is a wise and understanding people." For what great nation is there that has a god so near to it as the LORD our God is to us, whenever we call upon him? And what great nation is there, that has statutes and rules so righteous as all this law that I set before you today? (Deuteronomy 4:5–8)

While many Christians believe that believers in Jesus have supplanted or replaced the Jewish people in this role, the Jewish Jesus teaches us otherwise.[66] Rather than coming to do away with the chosenness of his people, Jesus came to empower them and to lead them to fulfill their mission. As his followers, it is our duty to come alongside the Jewish people in support of their God-given, irrevocable mission and calling: "As regards election, they are beloved for the sake of their forefathers. For the gifts and the calling of God are irrevocable" (Romans 11:28–29).

One of the ways in which we are commanded to do this is through material aid. It is not difficult to find opportunities to bless the Jewish people. There will never be a lack of need. Humanitarian organizations like Chevra represent incredible opportunities for Christians to make a positive difference in the lives of Jewish people, and to fulfill an ancient and powerful role that God-fearing Gentiles were given by the apostles themselves.

.

Principle 2
Embrace Discipline

*Rising very early in the morning, while it was
still dark, he departed and went out to a desolate
place, and there he prayed.*

— *Mark 1:35*

Part of understanding Jesus' Jewishness was, for me, understanding the intensely rigorous lifestyle that he embraced. As
a religious Jew, Jesus obeyed not only the 613 commandments of
the Torah (so far as they applied to him) but also a great number of
additional stringencies that had accumulated through centuries
of Jewish tradition.

Jesus' spiritual walk, his religious life, was structured. It was
full of rules and regulations.

Yet often when Christians today decide to embrace a life of
structure, of rules and regulations, they are labeled legalists.

Legalism is truly a dangerous practice. Legalism, the idea that
one can earn eternal life by doing good things, is a false teaching
that circumvents the grace of God. It is incompatible with the
gospel of Jesus Christ.

However, I have probably seen as much damage done in believers' spiritual lives from knee-jerk reactions against legalism as I
have seen from legalism itself.

In fact, as I look at what passes for Christianity in America today,
I would argue that we have swerved from the legalism ditch on one

side of the road and crashed firmly into the pit of anything-goes spiritualism on the other side. This obviously isn't true of every single believer or every single church, but in a broad organizational sense, the rigor and structure of American Christianity has been diluted and compromised. Our standards have fallen tremendously from the days in which the Apostle Paul could write, "Purge the evil person from among you" (1 Corinthians 5:13) over sins that are now hallmarks of church life in some congregations—sins such as slander and backbiting (1 Corinthians 5:11).

Many believers—particularly nondenominational Protestants— recoil at the idea that our spiritual lives should be structured or that the bar for entry into church life should be so high. Real spirituality is seen as spontaneous, "led by the Holy Spirit," and characterized by a grace that covers these "minor" sins. But surely no one would claim to be more spiritual or full of grace than Jesus.

As a religious Jew, Jesus prayed liturgical prayers at set times— three times a day (in addition to spontaneous personal prayers). He was forbidden to eat certain foods. He had to adhere to certain standards of dress. While we do not know if he fasted regularly, the *Didache*, a first-century discipleship manual for non-Jewish believers, mandates two fast days every week in parallel with Jewish tradition of that time period. That's two days a week with *no food*.

Jesus restricted his activity on the Sabbath and traveled to Jerusalem three times a year for religious holidays. He attended synagogue services with incredible regularity and would have given a hefty percentage of his income to the Temple and to the poor, whether directly or through buying food from farmers who had already tithed on their produce.

Jesus held his disciples to a high standard, telling them that they needed to be even more scrupulous than the highly observant scribes and Pharisees (Matthew 5:20).

Even this list of rules is only the tip of the iceberg. While we tend to think of Jesus as acting in seemingly random ways as the leading of the Spirit moved him, in reality his walk of faith was highly structured and based on a very careful reading of the Scriptures. And while he is perfect, and we are not, I don't think he has given us permission to aim for a lower target; we must be imitators of Christ (1 John 2:6).

We won't end up living *exactly* like Jesus, especially if we're not Jewish; the Bible doesn't require exactly the same things from Jews and Gentiles. Just as Jesus would have heard a portion of the Torah scroll every week and mentally distinguished between the commandments that applied only if one were a Levitical priest (which he wasn't) and the commandments that applied to every Jewish person (which he was), so we must distinguish between commandments that apply only to the Jewish people and commandments that apply to everyone, Jew or Gentile. Just as Jesus didn't have to observe all 613 commandments of the Torah, neither do his Gentile followers. In fact, because we are not under Jewish religious law, our burden is much lighter than his.[67]

But even though being like Jesus doesn't mean becoming Jewish, it *does* mean that we should be just as rigorous in spiritual things as he was. We must be just as intentional with our own spiritual formation, just as rigorous and structured as he was in his spiritual life.

Simply put, we have to start taking discipleship seriously and stop taking our salvation for granted.

While there are some widely read Christian authors—Deitrich Bonhoeffer, Dallas Willard, Richard Foster, and others—who have encouraged their readers to embrace rigor, discipline, and structure in their walks of faith, more voices must join that chorus. More churches must help their congregants to build this kind of structure and discipline into their lives.

We collectively need to set the bar higher—not for our culture, but for ourselves and our churches.

Principle 3
Kingdom Thinking

*The time is fulfilled, and the kingdom of God is
at hand; repent and believe in the gospel.*

— Mark 1:15

Another way in which Jesus' Jewishness has impacted my spiritual life has been in the way I understand the gospel, the message of salvation.

Before, I used to think that Jesus coming to die for my sins was the entire gospel message. I knew that he was coming back—but why? To take me to eternal bliss. I knew that he had risen from the dead—but why? To prove that my atonement had been secured. I knew all these things because of how they related to my own personal salvation.

But Jesus' message was not just about how people can go to heaven when they die. In fact, he talks about that subject surprisingly little, especially in the Gospels of Matthew, Mark, and Luke.

Jesus' message is way bigger than my personal salvation or your personal salvation or even the salvation of the church. It is about the redemption of the whole world, the restoration of the planet, the gleaming bright future that God promised through the Old Testament prophets. Every ill mended, every broken heart healed, poverty and corruption erased forever. These are the things that Jesus promised.

The term Jesus used to describe this idyllic future was the "kingdom of God" or the "kingdom of heaven" (these terms are synonymous; in Jesus' time, "heaven" was often used as another way to say "God").

Jesus' message is called the "gospel of the kingdom of heaven." It is the good news that God is going to repair the world.

When we embrace the gospel, we also embrace the responsibility of joining God in this reparation. We commit to making the kingdom a reality in our own lives—doing what we can to mend ills, heal broken hearts, and even end poverty and corruption when it is in our power to do so.

While the world will not truly enjoy the eternal bliss of the kingdom of heaven until Jesus returns, we can still give the world a taste of what that kingdom will be like through the way we live, the way we act, the way we treat others.

Unfortunately, in the early twentieth century, American Christianity split on this issue. Some Christians emphasized the "social gospel"—helping the destitute, feeding the poor, healing the sick— to the detriment of the message of personal discipleship to Jesus. Others downplayed the social elements of the gospel too much, pursuing only converts and ignoring the larger mission to repair the world.

This division is unnecessary and harmful. Both elements of the gospel are important and badly needed. We don't have to choose between telling people about Jesus and helping those who are in need. In fact, they are vitally connected. We can actually show people the love of Jesus Christ and draw them closer to him by making the world around us a little more like the kingdom that is coming. As we do this, we can also be straightforward about the salvation from sin and death that comes to those who follow Jesus.

Principle 4
Bring Restoration

*I have great sorrow and unceasing anguish in
my heart. For I could wish that I myself were
accursed and cut off from Christ for the sake of
my brothers, my kinsmen according to the flesh.*

— Romans 9:2–3

The church has a blind spot where their vision of the Jewish Jesus should be.[68] This blind spot has caused more problems than we can imagine. One of these problems is the fact that we have made Jesus unrecognizable as the Messiah.

The religious Jewish community has clear expectations of the Messiah. These expectations are based on multitudes of promises and prophecies recorded in the Old Testament. The Messiah will come and restore his people (Isaiah 11:11–12). He will bring them back to their land (Jeremiah 30:3). He will enforce the Law of Moses with righteousness and justice (Isaiah 2:2–4).

The traditional Christian perception of Jesus is that he will not do these things. Instead of restoring his people, he abandoned them for a new people. Instead of the Jewish people being brought back to their land, they were banished from their land. Instead of enforcing the Law of Moses, the traditional Jesus annulled it.

By holding up this traditional picture of Jesus, so radically different from the historical Jesus in these key areas, we have made it almost impossible for a religious Jew to believe that Jesus is the

Messiah. Those who did believe are mostly not Jewish anymore; for most of the past two thousand years, essentially all Jews who overcame these barriers and converted to Christianity lost their Jewish identity.

They didn't just lose their history, their traditions, and their Torah. They lost the very fact that they were Jewish. They assimilated into non-Jewish society. They became Gentiles, in direct contravention of the Apostle Paul's "rule in all the churches": "Was anyone at the time of his call already circumcised? Let him not seek to remove the marks of circumcision" (1 Corinthians 7:17–18). (In that time "circumcision" meant "Jewish" or "conversion to Judaism.")[69]

Observant Jews mourn over what has happened to their brothers who have accepted Jesus. It has meant the destruction, the annihilation, the complete loss of their Jewish identity. These Jewish believers have "removed the marks of circumcision"—removed everything about their lives that identified them as Jewish.[70] Can this be the result of the work of the Messiah, who is supposed to restore his people, bring them back to their land, and enforce the Law of Moses?

When Christians forgot that Jesus was Jewish, we closed the door for the Jewish people to corporately recognize that Jesus is their Messiah. While I believe the "stumbling" of Israel was part of God's plan (Romans 11:11–32), Christians are still going to be held accountable for "shutting the kingdom of heaven in people's faces" (see Matthew 23:13) by holding up a Jesus that is unrecognizable as the Messiah to the Jewish people.

This is a harsh indictment. But I think we deserve it.

Think about it. If it were somehow possible for Christians all over the world to see the same Jesus, to see the Jewish Jesus, and to lift that historically accurate Jesus up for the whole world to see, would he not "draw all people" to himself (John 12:32)?

We aren't responsible for the way people respond to Jesus. We can't change someone's heart, and we can't draw them to God—God does these things (John 6:44; 1 Corinthians 3:5–7).

But we *are* responsible to be truthful and accurate. As the "body of Christ" (1 Corinthians 12:27), it is our responsibility to show the world what Jesus is like. If we are going to represent Jesus, we must get our facts straight. We must show the world a historically accurate picture of Jesus. If we don't, we "put a stumbling block before the blind" (Leviticus 19:14). We cause people to misunderstand and reject Jesus because we're not showing them the right Jesus to begin with.

We must repair the damage. We must cure the sickness. Not only for our sake, but for the sake of the Jewish people and for the sake of all those who do not yet know Jesus. We must meet Jesus—Rabbi Yeshua of Nazareth—afresh and anew. We must let him restore our homes, our churches, our denominations, our world.

This will only happen if you and I take an active role in helping people understand who Jesus was and is. Denominations, churches, publishing ministries, and seminaries change slowly—but they do change, one person at a time. It's up to us to win souls, change hearts, and bring understanding so that Jesus can break in and bring healing and renewal.

We must prepare the way before him so that when the time comes, his people will see him for who he really is.

Fortify

This final principle has another dimension that conservative Christians may want to take special note of.

University-based theological and biblical scholars in the past hundred years or so have mostly abandoned the traditional Christian idea of who Jesus was and is. Part of this process has been the stripping away of all supernatural elements from the story of Jesus. Many believe, based on what we hold as the basic principles of modern science, that Jesus could not have done the miracles that the Gospels attribute to him. Others have even gone so far as to teach that the historical person of Jesus—a miraculous God-man—just doesn't make any sense, and probably didn't exist at all.

This movement in the universities has percolated into popular culture quite successfully. It is increasingly true that people don't really take the traditional Jesus seriously anymore.

Christians have reacted in different ways to this abandonment of the traditional Jesus by university scholars and by the broader culture. Many Christians simply reject university scholarship that does not agree with their views. Others, however, have responded to these scholars on their own terms. For example, Rudolf Bultmann took up the challenge of secular scholars and retold the story of Jesus through a process he called "demythologization."

Demythologizing the Gospels, for Bultmann, meant reinterpreting the miracle stories of Jesus to mean something different than literal miracles. He taught that Jesus' disciples, so moved by his life and teaching, told miracle stories about him in order to communicate deeper truths. Bultmann, a Christian, was convinced that by removing the literal miracles from the Gospels, he was making the story of Jesus accessible to people who could not believe in both miracles and science. However, in the process he had to argue that the Gospels were not useful or reliable as historical documents—in other words, we can't be sure that any of what they tell us really happened apart from the exercise of blind faith.

Bultmann was probably the most influential theologian of the twentieth century. His views, or views that are based on his work, are still taught in seminaries all over the world. Many pastors and other Christians really believe that the Gospels need to be demythologized in order to make sense. But demythologization rejects some of the most essential and basic elements of our faith. If God couldn't break into history and work miracles in the past, how do we believe he will save us in the future?

Christianity is, at its core, a religion based on the belief that a real person came back from the dead. If that didn't happen, there is no reason for us to keep believing. Paul taught this in 1 Corinthians 15, the most detailed chapter in the Bible on the resurrection from the dead: "If Christ has not been raised, then our preaching is in vain and your faith is in vain. … If Christ has not been raised, your faith is futile and you are still in your sins. … If in Christ we have hope in this life only, we are of all people most to be pitied" (1 Corinthians 15:14, 17, 19).

However, many believers feel that they have no other option but to follow Bultmann and radically reinterpret the Gospels. They haven't found any other way to make the Gospels seem believable in today's world. They think that the Gospels just don't make any sense as real historical documents. They say, "We just have to take Jesus' existence on faith. We have no real evidence."

Many conservative scholars, on the other hand, have reacted by retrenching, by digging in their heels. Fundamentalist and evangelical Christians have their own universities and their own scholarship dedicated to disproving scholars like Bultmann. But they are not taking ground. The scholars on the far right wing of this movement are so committed to the traditional view of Jesus—a person who happened to be Jewish but came to end Judaism—that they refuse to give one inch to the world of historical Jesus scholarship. Because of this, their interpretation of the Gospels is full of holes. It is easy for other scholars to ignore them. The rest of the academic world simply knows too much about Jesus and Judaism to see a non-Jewish Jesus.

But when we read the Gospels as Jewish literature about a Jewish rabbi, they make far more sense, and they are far more believable as historical documents. Much that is strange or puzzling about Jesus becomes clear and makes sense when we realize that we are reading about a Jewish rabbi of the Second Temple Period. Scholars who realize this have argued that even someone who does not believe in miracles must still take the Gospels seriously as Jewish literature—and as historical documentation.[71]

This is just one specific example of how embracing Jesus' Jewish identity strengthens and reinforces the faith of the believer. Knowing Jesus in his humanity and in his Jewishness helps us to connect the historical Jesus (the flesh-and-blood person who walked the earth) and the Jesus of our faith (the Son of God and Savior of the world) as one person. It gives us confidence that Jesus really did walk the earth two thousand years ago, because the stories told about him have the ring of historical truth—even though sometimes they may seem unbelievable.

With the Jewish Jesus as our touchstone, we can better hold our ground in the academic world. As researchers learn more about Second Temple Judaism and more about the Gospels, it is getting harder and harder to claim that Jesus never existed or that the Gospels don't portray the real life of a real person.

However, it is also getting harder and harder to claim that Jesus got rid of the Torah, or that his disciples didn't practice Judaism, or that the early church wasn't completely Jewish in character.

As Jesus scholarship matures, and as more scholars recognize that Jesus was a practicing Jewish rabbi with practicing Jewish disciples, our faith actually finds firmer footing—that is, if we are ready to stake our entire destiny on Yeshua, the Rabbi from Nazareth.

If not, if we cannot accept the Jewish Jesus, if we choose the Jesus of church tradition instead, then the world of archaeology and research threatens to swallow us up. As our culture becomes better educated in these areas, our evangelistic efforts will stop bearing fruit.

If we have to make potential converts choose between our theological image of Jesus and the real historical Jesus, if a lost person has to reject the entire world of Jesus scholarship in order to believe in the Jesus whom the church is offering, then we had better get ready to hear "no" for an answer.

But if we can accept that which is good and right in historical Jesus scholarship, and if we can accept what our own records—the Jewish books that we collected and called the New Testament—say about Jesus and his followers, we will put our faith on solid ground.

It really is do or die. In the end, we can have the risen Rabbi or no Jesus at all.

A Final Word

My hope is built on nothing less
Than Jesus' blood and righteousness.

I dare not trust the sweetest frame,
But wholly lean on Jesus' name.

On Christ, the solid Rock, I stand;
All other ground is sinking sand.

— *Edward Mote*

Christians generally understand that they should be like Jesus Christ, but most of us don't know enough about Jesus to make this aspect of discipleship a daily reality in our lives.

There is no Christianity without Jesus Christ. He is at the center of everything we believe in. He is our connection with God. We literally worship and adore him.

But we hardly know anything about him.

How can we be like someone we don't know anything about?

Think about it for a while, and even scarier questions begin to emerge. What if Jesus isn't anything like what most of us think?

What if the real Jesus doesn't look anything like the stained-glass windows and children's book illustrations? Even worse—what if we're not really following his teachings? What if Jesus wouldn't agree with either of our political parties' platforms? What if the core of his message is different than we think it is? What if we think we are doing a great job following him but in reality we would have been kicked out of the Upper Room?

What if we have lost a really biblical idea of who Jesus is?

Pick up and open any popular book on American Christianity and you'll read about problems. The church has problems. Christianity has problems. We aren't functioning correctly. In some way, we're broken; we're sick. People are leaving churches, youth aren't keeping their faith into their college years, pastors are suffering from burnout, and church doors are closing all over the country.

Some of our churches are experiencing great numerical success, but statisticians like George Barna remind us that even as the majority of Americans claim to have had a conversion experience, and even as some churches experience huge growth, only a tiny fraction of professed believers are truly committed to the faith, and most churches are struggling. If anything, the Western church appears to be shrinking. We're getting weaker, smaller. Slowly but surely, we're circling the drain.

Spare me the Bible verses about the narrow path that few find. I have read the New Testament, and the New Testament church wasn't sick or dying. It grew exponentially. It rocked its world. It set in motion a movement that now encompasses the globe. Why don't we generally see that kind of movement in the church down the street?

Every book I've read has a different solution. Maybe we don't love hard enough. Maybe we don't pray hard enough. Maybe we don't evangelize enough. Maybe we haven't fully grasped God's grace. Maybe we're not satisfied enough in God. Maybe we're not committed to making disciples. Maybe we have failed to engage the culture. Maybe we have forgotten what our mission is. And sure, these are all problems. But what is the source of these problems? Why aren't we doing all those things?

To me these problems sound like symptoms. The church at large hasn't found the real root of the issue, the real disease. Not yet.

I have been going to church for longer than I can remember. I have wondered, along with everyone else, what the problem is. Why doesn't our church look like Acts 2 or 1 Corinthians 13 or Philippians 4? Why aren't church attendees becoming converts, and why aren't converts becoming disciples? Why do people in church seem to complain so much? Why do they leave at the drop of a hat? What's with the backbiting and shallowness? Where's the depth? Where's the passion? Where's the commitment? Where's the community? Where's the love?

As committed Christians, we are so close to the answer. We are on the cusp of it. We are standing on the solution, and we don't even know it. We sing about it in church and hear about it from the pulpit.

The solution is Jesus, and the problem is that we have lost sight of who Jesus is.

Not only that, we have lost sight of so much of what Jesus came to do, of what Jesus' core message was, and even to whom Jesus' message was originally delivered.

In place of the real, living Jesus, we have substituted a theological formula, a set of beliefs, a litany of dogma. We have substituted the Apostles' Creed for the teachings of the apostles. We have substituted the Nicene Creed for the person of Christ. I am not saying that beliefs are bad—they are good, they are necessary, and Christians cannot afford to be slouches when it comes to theology—but theology and beliefs are no substitute for a real relationship with a real person, the real historical Jesus.

The only solution to Christianity's problem, the only cure for her illness, is to bring back a personal, intimate knowledge of Christ, to really encounter him, to meet him afresh, to get to know him as the first Christians did. We have to know Jesus better. If necessary, we have to sacrifice everything else in order to know Jesus better.

There is no other solution. There is no way to sustain a Christianity that is not fully, completely centered on the historical person of Jesus Christ, and there is no way to center our lives on Jesus Christ if we don't take the time and effort to know Jesus as well as we possibly can.

Jesus is all we have—our only connection with the Father. If we get one thing right, it had better be Jesus.

"On Christ, the solid Rock, I stand; all other ground is sinking sand."

If you are a disciple of Christ, then wherever your spiritual journey takes you from here, it must be informed by an accurate conception of Jesus. The picture of Jesus in your mind must match the real historical person of Jesus. In this chaotic world full of differing and contradictory beliefs about Jesus, you cannot afford to be any less than crystal clear on the identity of Jesus of Nazareth.

Today, thanks to the efforts of centuries of biblical scholarship, we know that Jesus was a practicing Jew. We know that our faith is built on nothing less than the blood and righteousness of a Jewish rabbi from a backwater town in Israel.

And I think this matters. Yeshua matters. The fact that Jesus was a practicing Jew matters. It changes how we see him, how we hear his teachings, how we follow him. It changes how we see ourselves and how we see his people, the Jewish people. It changes how we live and how we do church. It changes our message. Or at least it should.

In this book I have tried to give you an idea of exactly how Jesus' Jewishness has begun to impact my life of faith. I hope it is a good starting point for you, but I can't be sure exactly what all this will mean for you in your situation. All I can say is that you must consider it, weigh it, meditate on it, and work out its implications for yourself. Ignorance and inaction are not viable options.

Consider Hebrews 1:1–2: "Long ago, at many times and in many ways, God spoke to our fathers by the prophets, but in these last days he has spoken to us by his Son, whom he appointed the heir of all things, through whom also he created the world."

God has spoken; God has revealed himself through the historical person of Jesus, through Rabbi Yeshua of Nazareth. God, to put it another way, has already done his job.

Now it's up to us. It's time to get serious. It's time to get to know Jesus better.

Endnotes

1   This is the general conclusion of at least one major wing of what is today called "the third quest for the historical Jesus." Many, many books have been written on the different "quests" that have been undertaken over the past two hundred years to recover the historical person of Jesus from behind the texts of the Gospels. The "first quest," a term now used to describe historical Jesus scholarship up to the early twentieth century, was summarized by Albert Schweitzer in his famous book *The Quest of the Historical Jesus*, originally published in German in 1906. The 1910 English translation is in the public domain and is instructive reading in its own right. However, the quest didn't stop with Schweitzer. The "second quest," undertaken by historical Jesus scholars of the mid-twentieth century and informed by the theology of Rudolf Bultmann, attempted to see Jesus as radically different from his Jewish background. With the third quest, however, and the past four decades of intense research, Jesus scholarship has matured to the point at which we can safely make the statement cited here, broadly referencing, in no particular order, Gerd Thiessen, Amy-Jill Levine, David Flusser, Paula Fredriksen, Richard Bauckham, Geza Vermes, E.P. Sanders, Bruce Chilton, Craig Evans, Dale Allison, and others for scholarly support.

2   See the above citation.

3   The village described here is based on excavations of Cana (Khirbet Qana). See Peter Richardson, "Khirbet Qana (and Other Villages) as a Context for Jesus" in *Jesus and Archaeology* (ed. James H. Charlesworth; Grand Rapids, MI: Eerdmans, 2006), 120–44; Joshua Schwartz, "Jesus the 'Material Jew'" in *The Jewish Jesus: Revelation, Reflection, Reclamation* (ed. Zev Garber; West Lafayette, IN: Purdue University Press, 2011), 47–64. The synagogue description was in addition informed by E. P. Sanders, *The Historical Figure of Jesus* (London, England: Penguin, 1993), 98–101, in which Sanders argues that the paucity of archaeological evidence for first-century synagogue buildings (in contrast to their ubiquity in texts from

and about the time period) can be explained by the fact that later buildings were often built on top of them, and archaeologists are often not able to access the earlier structures presumed to be underneath. The account itself is a fictionalized version of Luke 13:10–16.

4   Stuart Dauermann, *Son of David: Healing the Vision of the Messianic Jewish Movement* (Eugene, OR: Wipf & Stock, 2010), 3.

5   Note that the Pharisees, though they have a reputation for being overly strict, actually *relaxed* the purity laws somewhat to put them within the reach of the common people. See Roland Deines, "Biblical Views: The Pharisees—Good Guys with Bad Press," *Biblical Archaeology Review* 39:04 (2013).

6   John Dominic Crossan and Jonathan L. Reed, *Excavating Jesus: Beneath the Stones, Behind the Texts* (New York, NY: HarperCollins, 2001), 208.

7   Yitzhak Magen, "Ancient Israel's Stone Age: Purity in Second Temple Times," *Biblical Archeology Review* 24:05 (1998), 46–52, an article brought to my attention by Toby Janicki in a lecture entitled "True and False Purity."

8   D. Thomas Lancaster, *Torah Club: Chronicles of the Messiah*, (Marshfield, MO: First Fruits of Zion, 2014), xi.

9   t.*Shabbat* 1.4.

10   See Magen, "Ancient Israel's Stone Age."

11   There are exceptions. Contrast, for example, some of the older commentaries on James with the newer commentary by Scot McKnight, which is highly readable and makes use of recent scholarship on the early Jewish church and the state of Judaism in the time of James.

12   The cheap and free (public domain) lexicons and dictionaries usually fall into this category—Brown-Driver-Briggs, Thayer's, and Genesius, for example, all predate some important archaeological discoveries.

13   The massive *Theological Dictionary of the New Testament* would be a prime example here. While it is a useful and comprehensive resource, it unapologetically stands within a very particular theological stream of thought.

14   For example, see Craig Evans' defense of Jesus' Jewishness and his critique of Burton Mack's characterization of Jesus as a Cynic philosopher in "The Misplaced Jesus: Interpreting Jesus in a Judaic Context," in *The Missing Jesus: Rabbinic Judaism and the New Testament* (ed. Bruce Chilton, Craig A. Evans, and Jacob Neusner; Boston, MA: Brill, 2002), 11–39. Through hundreds of similar books and articles, Evans and other scholars have spent decades placing the weight of evidence on the side of a practicing Jewish Jesus.

15 I am not the first person to make this comparison; see, for example, Peter Enns, *Inspiration and Incarnation: Evangelicals and the Problem of the Old Testament* (Grand Rapids, MI: Baker, 2005).

16 Luke 13:1 records one such incident in which Pontius Pilate had a group of Galilean protestors clubbed to death.

17 Lancaster, *Torah Club: Chronicles of the Messiah*, 1628.

18 Sanders, *Historical Figure of Jesus*, 48: "All Jews ... believed that they should understand the divine law and obey it."

19 As described in m.*Avot* 5.22.

20 Sanders, *Historical Figure of Jesus*, 37–38: "'Religion' in Judaism ... encompassed all of life. ... *Judaism elevated all of life to the same level as worship of God*" (emphasis in original).

21 This and further details can be found in Alfred Edersheim, *The Life and Times of Jesus the Messiah* (Grand Rapids, MI: Eerdmans, 1971), 221–34.

22 Justin Martyr, *Dialogue with Trypho* 88, records an early tradition that Jesus built plows and yokes.

23 Matthew 11:19; Mark 2:15–17; John 2:1–11.

24 D. Thomas Lancaster, *Torah Club: Chronicles of the Messiah*, 200. For another author who has connected Jesus with Ezekiel's chariot vision, see Bruce Chilton, *Rabbi Jesus: An Intimate Biography: The Jewish Life and Teaching that Inspired Christianity* (New York, NY: Doubleday, 2000), 50–57.

25 There are differing interpretations of the purpose of the Sermon on the Mount. Here we follow, among others, Geza Vermes, *The Religion of Jesus the Jew* (Minneapolis, MN: Fortress, 1993), 30–37; W.D. Davies, *The Setting of the Sermon on the Mount* (Cambridge, England: Cambridge University Press, 1964), 425–35; Amy-Jill Levine, *The Misunderstood Jew: The Church and the Scandal of the Jewish Jesus* (New York, NY: HarperOne, 2006), 47; Amy-Jill Levine and Marc Zvi Brettler, eds., *The Jewish Annotated New Testament* (New York, NY: Oxford University Press, 2011), 11: "The common term 'antitheses' (lit., 'oppositions') for these six teachings is inaccurate; some teachings proclaim not antithesis, but intensification (comparable to 'making a fence around the Torah'; see m.*Avot* 1.1)."

26 Andreas J. Köstenberger, *Encountering John: The Gospel in Historical, Literary, and Theological Perspective* (Grand Rapids, MI: Baker, 1999), 137.

27 Some would dispute the appropriateness of the use of the word "rabbi" to describe Jesus. Jacob Neusner, for example, wrote that Jesus doesn't qualify as a rabbi according to the standards of rabbinic Judaism because he did not pass forward the *mesorah*, the body of

Jewish oral teaching, as he received it—see his *Questions and Answers: Intellectual Foundations of Judaism* (Peabody, MA: Hendrickson, 2005), 27. We must also remind the reader that the definition of "rabbi" in the Amoraic period was different than it was in later periods and that to use the term of Jesus in his time period would have carried a different meaning than it does today (Chilton, *Rabbi Jesus*, 296). Here we stand with Chilton and others who point out that the primary sources indicate that in his time Jesus was in fact recognized as a rabbi in the first-century sense of the word—that is, as a teacher of Judaism.

28 Lancaster, *Torah Club: Chronicles of the Messiah*, 212.

29 Sanders, *Historical Figure of Jesus*, 43.

30 m.*Peah* 1.1; for sources for the one sixtieth lower limit, see commentary in *The ArtScroll Mishnah Series: Seder Zeraim*, vol. 2(a), *Peah* (Brooklyn, NY: Mesorah, 1990), 16.

31 Josephus, *Jewish War* 2.8.14.

32 Jesus wasn't the only Jewish teacher to point out the fact that many Pharisees didn't live up to their own standards; see b.*Sotah* 22b.

33 m.*Avot* 1.1 dates the command to make disciples back to the time of Ezra. See Lancaster, *Torah Club: Chronicles of the Messiah*, iv.

34 These responsibilities of a disciple are taken from Lancaster, *Torah Club: Chronicles of the Messiah*, iv.

35 This same question appears in the Mishnah in tractate *Nedarim* 9.1, and, incidentally, the Jewish leadership ended up siding with Jesus. See Lancaster, *Torah Club: Chronicles of the Messiah*, 755.

36 m.*Avot* 1.1.

37 Lancaster, *Torah Club: Chronicles of the Messiah*, 691.

38 Based on an interpretation of Mark 4:11–12 and Matthew 13:13. This interpretation is addressed from a Jewish perspective in R. Steven Notley and Ze'ev Safrai, *Parables of the Sages: Jewish Wisdom from Jesus to Rav Ashi* (Jerusalem, Israel: Carta, 2011), 28–31.

39 Lancaster, *Torah Club: Chronicles of the Messiah*, 587–88.

40 Paula Fredriksen, *Augustine and the Jews: A Christian Defense of Jews and Judaism* (New York, NY: Doubleday, 2008), 3–102.

41 The terms "bind" and "loose" are technical terms in Judaism. They mean "forbid" and "permit," respectively. See Lancaster, *Torah Club: Chronicles of the Messiah*, 792.

42 See Ben Witherington III, *Letters and Homilies for Jewish Christians: A Socio-Rhetorical Commentary on Hebrews, James and Jude* (Downers Grove, IL: InterVarsity Press, 2007).

43 To understand why Matthew is omitted from this list, consider Anthony J. Saldarini, *Matthew's Christian-Jewish Community* (Chicago, IL: University of Chicago Press, 1994).

44 This does not mean that we can't reconstruct Paul's theology, but we must do so carefully. See James D.G. Dunn, *The Theology of Paul the Apostle* (Grand Rapids, MI: Eerdmans, 1998). Dunn explains the difficulty and then undertakes the task.

45 One of many authors to argue this point (that Paul wrote only to Gentiles) is Caroline Johnson Hodge, *If Sons, Then Heirs: A Study of Kinship and Ethnicity in the Letters of Paul* (New York, NY: Oxford University Press, 2007), 9–11; see also Krister Stendahl, *Paul Among Jews and Gentiles* (Minneapolis, MN: Fortress, 1976).

46 D. Thomas Lancaster, *What About the Sacrifices?* (Marshfield, MO: First Fruits of Zion, 2011), 2.

47 Lancaster, *What About the Sacrifices?* 6–9.

48 Lancaster, *What About the Sacrifices?* 16–17.

49 Gordon Wenham, *Word Biblical Commentary*, vol. 1, *Genesis 1–15* (Nashville, TN: Thomas Nelson, 1987), 138–43.

50 David J.A. Clines, *Word Biblical Commentary*, vol. 17, *Job 1–20* (Nashville, TN: Thomas Nelson, 1989), 18–19.

51 These psalms are further explored in Daniel Boyarin's *The Jewish Gospels: The Story of the Jewish Christ* (New York, NY: The New Press, 2012), 28–29.

52 Ibid.

53 This perspective on "Son of God" and its development as a title for Jesus was informed by Geza Vermes, *Jesus the Jew: A Historian's Reading of the Gospels* (Philadelphia, PA: Fortress, 1981), 192–213.

54 The concept of the king of any given people being titled "son of God" was not unique to Judaism. See Paula Fredricksen, "Compassion Is to Purity as Fish Is to Bicycle" in *Apocalypticism, Anti-Semitism and the Historical Jesus: Subtexts in Criticism*, ed. John S. Kloppenborg (New York, NY: Bloomsbury T&T Clark, 2005), 57–58.

55 Not all anthropomorphisms were removed in the Aramaic Targums, and there is considerable scholarly debate on exactly what the connection is between the *Memra* and anthropomorphization. Suffice it to say that there is almost certainly some connection.

56 For a cogent and recent argument for this position, see John Ronning, *The Jewish Targums and John's Logos Theology* (Grand Rapids, MI: Baker, 2010).

57 *Dialogue with Trypho* 11.

58 *Dialogue with Trypho* 16–23.

59 John Chrysostom, *Treatise on the Priesthood*, IV.4.

60 We know this because Gentiles were not allowed in the Temple. See Acts 21:28, in which Paul is wrongfully accused of bringing a non-Jew into the Temple.

61 For a history of these believing Jews, see Oskar Skarsaune and Reidar Hvalvik, eds., *Jewish Believers in Jesus: The Early Centuries* (Peabody, MA: Hendrickson, 2007).

62 Narrative condensed from Lancaster, *Torah Club: Chronicles of the Messiah*; see also David Flusser, *The Sage from Galilee: Rediscovering Jesus' Genius* (Grand Rapids, MI: Eerdmans, 2007), 154.

63 George Barna, *Growing True Disciples: New Strategies for Producing Genuine Followers of Christ* (Colorado Springs, CO: Waterbrook, 2001), 43.

64 "'Nones' on the Rise," Pew Research Center, n.p. [cited 9 December 2013]. Online: http://www.pewforum.org/2012/10/09/nones-on-the-rise/.

65 Larry Shannon-Missal, "Americans Belief in God, Miracles and Heaven Declines," The Harris Poll #97, n.p. [cited 18 December 2013]. Online: http://www.harrisinteractive.com/NewsRoom/HarrisPolls/tabid/447/ctl/ReadCustom%20Default/mid/1508/ArticleId/1353/Default.aspx.

66 Probably the most powerful Christian statement to this effect was made by R. Kendall Soulen in his book *The God of Israel and Christian Theology* (Minneapolis, MN: Fortress, 1996). See also Mark S. Kinzer, *Postmissionary Messianic Judaism: Redefining Christian Engagement with the Jewish People* (Grand Rapids, MI: Brazos, 2005); Lev Gillet, *Communion in the Messiah* (London, England: Lutterworth, 1942).

67 See Toby Janicki, *God-Fearers: Gentiles and the God of Israel* (Marshfield, MO: First Fruits of Zion, 2012).

68 I borrow language here from Dauermann, *Son of David*, 3.

69 Mark Nanos, *The Irony of Galatians: Paul's Letter in First-Century Context* (Minneapolis, MN: Fortress, 2002), 88 –91.

70 See David J. Rudolph, "Paul's 'Rule in All the Churches' (1 Cor. 7:17–24) and Torah-Defined Ecclesiological Variegation," paper presented at the American Academy of Religion Conference, 3 November 2008 [cited 10 December 2013]. Online: http://ejournals.bc.edu/ojs/index.php/scjr/article/view/1556/. The "marks of circumcision" are markers of Jewish identity such as dietary laws and Sabbath keeping.

71 Richard Bauckham goes into great detail on the historical reliability of the Gospels as eyewitness accounts of a Jewish rabbi in *Jesus and the Eyewitnesses: The Gospels as Eyewitness Testimony* (Grand Rapids, MI: Eerdmans, 2008).

About the Author

J acob Fronczak has spent the past fifteen years ministering in local churches in numerous support and leadership roles. He completed his M.Div. through Liberty University in 2013 and is currently the lead pastor at Eastpoint Community Church in Coldwater, Michigan.

A member of First Fruits of Zion's creative team, Jacob is also a vocal supporter of the modern-day Messianic Jewish renewal, and has contributed to Messianic dialogue through contributions to *Messiah Journal* and *Kesher*. He believes Messianic Judaism has a critical role in connecting twenty-first-century Christianity with its first-century Jewish roots.